Putting Assessment for Learning into Practice

Also available in the Ideas in Action Series

Behaviour Management – Tony Swainston

Encouraging Reading – Susan Elkin

Creative Assemblies – Brian Radcliffe

Creating an Inclusive School – Mal Leicester

Effective Learning – Gavin Reid and Shannon Green

Emotional Literacy – David Spendlove

Teaching NLP in the Classroom - Kate Spohrer

Also available from Continuum

Assessment: A Guide for Secondary Teachers – Howard Tanner and Sonia Jones

Assessment – Margaret Sangster and Lynn Overall

An Introduction to Assessment – Patricia Broadfoot

Putting Assessment for Learning into Practice

David Spendlove

Ideas in Action

continuum

Canterbury College

103590

Continuum International Publishing Group

The Tower Building
11 York Road
London SE1 7NX

80 Maiden Lane
Suite 704
New York NY 10038

www.continuumbooks.com

Reprinted 2010, 2011 (three times)

British Library Cataloguing-in-Publication Data
A catalogue record for this book is available from the British Library.

ISBN: 9781847064103 (paperback)

Library of Congress Cataloging-in-Publication Data
Spendlove, David.
Putting assessment for learning into practice/David Spendlove.
p. cm. – (Ideas in action)
ISBN 978-1-84706-410-3 (pbk.)
1. Educational tests and measurements – Great Britain. 2. Effective teaching – Great Britain. 3. Learning – Great Britain. I. Title.
LB3056.G7S64 2009
372.260941–dc22

2008056041

Typeset by Newgen Imaging Systems Pvt Ltd, Chennai, India
Printed and bound in Great Britain

This book is dedicated to my best teachers:

Graham Watt
Bill Irlam
Geoff Crowley
John Spendlove
William Spendlove

Every student can learn,
just not on the same day,
or in the same way.

Contents

Introduction

Over the years I have interviewed hundreds of applicants wanting to study an undergraduate or postgraduate course to become a teacher. Not once in all those years, when asked the question 'why do you want to be a teacher?' has anyone answered 'because I am really interested in and good at assessment!' Candidates will often talk about wanting to work with children, which is positive, but when probed about how they will know when a child is learning the standard answer is 'give them an exam'. This is not a weakness on the part of the applicants; it is merely a reflection of their limited understanding, mostly from experiences as a pupil, of assessment. What's more, the generation of learners who were statutorily assessed (you may be one of them) in England at the ages of 5, 7, 11, 14, 16, 17 and 18 – the most assessed generation ever – are now entering the profession, often still regarding this bombardment of summative assessment as legitimate.

Somewhere in the evolution of education, assessment as the means for enhancing learning became distorted to become assessment for bureaucratic, recording and accountability reasons: a means of testing the teachers as much as the learners. As such, in the last decade we have witnessed the development of one of the most atomized assessment systems in the world, which has had a profound effect upon how teachers teach and what and how pupils learn. Alongside this is the added accountability of league tables and performativity, which has contributed to the intense effect of forcing teachers to teach to the test.

Such is the high stakes testing impact on teaching that many have described this as the 'technicization' of teaching where teachers have become deskilled and lack some autonomy in the classroom. It has become so much the norm that many teachers no longer trust their own judgement and prefer to rely upon the statutory tests to inform them of pupils' capabilities rather than the other way around – leading to the claims of 'over-schooled and under-educated'. In addition, Ofsted have also said that assessment is consistently the weakest part of teaching with only just over a third of schools being reasonably good at assessment.

This book, however, is not simply an attack on testing; it is a reminder of the big picture about the purpose of teaching and assessment as a means of ensuring deep, maximized, engaged and challenging learning and a reminder that testing tells us something – but not everything – and that assessment exists in many different forms.

> *Using one assessment for a multitude of purposes is like using a hammer for everything from brain-surgery to pile-driving.*
> *Haney (1991)*

The simple message is: good teaching can overcome bad testing and central to *assessment for learning* (AfL) is empowering learners through developing learning autonomy. This means involving learners in their own learning not just through reflection but also as co-constructors and co-negotiators of their learning.

Although this should lead to increased attainment, it is about much more than this. This is because learning represents a great deal more than that which can always be easily measured (ever tried to grade a sunset or a child's smile?). Therefore, although AfL should increase attainment, it is much more significant than that as it is central to learner empowerment and the development of an appetite for genuine lifelong learning.

I was once told the story of someone whose father was having heart problems. When their father went to see the heart specialist, he said that he could operate there and then. However, such were the advances in new forms of medicine and surgery that as the condition wasn't life threatening it would be much better to wait a year and use the new procedures which would greatly increase the patient's longevity.

I have often wondered about the equivalent scenario in education: 'I could assess you now but we are learning so much more, and I am getting so much better at assessment, that I realize I might get your assessment wrong and damage your life chances. However, if you wait a year there is a much greater chance of my being correct and the information I give you of being a real benefit.'

The reality is that in education new methods are coming along all the time but we don't appear to have the luxury of recognizing the weaknesses of existing systems and placing them on hold while we get it right. Instead we carry on using the same outdated methods, often knowing they may be doing some damage but also knowing that they work for some learners. Therefore central to AfL is a clear philosophy about doing the right thing; this means that teachers become formative teachers – that is, they shape their teaching to maximum effect to enhance all learners and they integrate AfL within the multitude of other activities essential to developing a rounded education. So while this book is about AfL, it is important that it links with the other key pieces of your personal educational jigsaw.

AfL in education

Traditionally we have accepted that assessment in education should predominantly be summative, such as end of unit tests, marks out of ten or yes/no answers. These can be useful but because they tend to be at the end of the process they don't tell you what you don't know at a time when you need to know what you don't know. They also, most significantly, don't tell you how to get better and as a result tend to encourage shallow, narrow teaching and learning leading to teaching to the test and superficial, constrained learning.

This type of teaching has generally been labelled as transmissionist: I have the knowledge; I decide what's important; I pass it on to you; you recall it and I tell you how well you did but not how you can improve. While this works for some teachers and some learners it isn't particularly effective for all learners. AfL instead front-loads and prioritizes the learning. It involves having most of the learners thinking most of the time and reduces the burden of regular testing by building in the assessment. AfL also suggests that if you know you have taught something effectively and you know something has been learned, then why is there a need to test at the end of the process when it is too late? AfL moves away from superficial approaches and places understanding as central to learning. Therefore teaching is differentiated and adjusted to learning and learning is managed to ensure genuine understanding.

> *AfL is the process of seeking and interpreting evidence for use by learners and their teachers to decide where the learners are in their learning, where they need to go and how best to get there.*
> Assessment Reform Group (2002)

Who is this book for?

This book is for all teachers and school leaders who are committed to ensuring learners are engaged in successful, meaningful and deep learning. Effective strategies based upon good practice are identified that place teachers and learners as central to the intelligent process of owning and adapting their teaching and learning process. This is to ensure that all learners can genuinely understand rather than merely recall what they have been taught.

Finally a warning: There is a danger that in using some of the strategies in this book that the big picture might be missed. AfL isn't just a series of strategies for increasing participation as a quick fix – it is a genuine commitment to clarifying and improving children's learning and as such is one part of a myriad of complex factors that influence both learning and attainment. Therefore the individual strategies in this book will have some effect on teaching and learning but AfL will only have a true effect when adopted as part of a personal and whole school philosophy.

Putting Assessment for Learning into Practice

1 Feedback and learning

There are only two questions needed

Some years ago I wrote an article for *The Times Educational Supplement* called 'There are only two questions' (you can read it in full in *The TES* archive). In it I suggested, slightly tongue-in-cheek, that all assessment, all the bureaucracy and accountability, could be reduced to two simple questions which took place on the pupil's last day of school. The two questions were:

Have you enjoyed your education so far?
Do you want to carry on learning when you leave school?

I still think that these are two very important questions; the point was to gauge not what pupils had retained but how much optimism they had for the future based upon their learning experiences – something we seemed to have lost sight of. Unfortunately, I suspect the answer from many children to both questions would be 'no' when the whole purpose of education should be for them to answer 'yes'. The reality is that that we know schools now operate under an immense amount of scrutiny through comparing pupils' results and distorting the role of assessment. Not all of this accountability is bad, however; a promotion of 'AfL' promotes assessment for the right purpose, which is prioritizing pupils' learning rather than accountability and restores autonomy back to teachers as 'conductors of learning'.

Advice

Feedback is central to AfL. However, instead of it being a one-way street, AfL has feedback from teacher to learner and learner to teacher with the feedback being a real time dialogue focusing upon learner improvement.

What do you want?

Before you dig in and start reading this book from cover to cover, it is important to decide how you most want to use this book – in effect you need to decide what your desired outcomes are. Knowing what you want at the start means you are more likely to achieve your goals through reading the book.

Possible ways of using this book	Yes	No	Maybe
To use as an introduction to the topic for yourself and follow up the further reading section?			
To use a page as the basis of a discussion in each of your staff meetings across the year?			
To use as a focus for departmental change?			
To use the book as a focus of an inset day?			
To use selected activities with children in lessons?			
To use as part of developing a policy on AfL?			
To split the book up across different subjects and years as part of a mapping exercise for AfL across the school?			
To use as a basis for educating parents (e.g. through newsletters) about the merits of AfL?			

Activity

Summative, formative and AfL

You will see throughout this book that central to AfL is the concept of formative assessment – that is assessment for enhancing and shaping learning through modifying teaching. This does not mean that summative assessments, assessment of learning, are all bad. It simply highlights that we have often got the emphasis, for a whole variety of cultural and historical reasons, the wrong way around. Formative assessment, as the name implies, shapes the learning process and is implicit in AfL. If the formative assessment does not, however, have an immediate impact in adjusting the teaching and learning, in that it is used for longer term adjustments, then it is not AfL. AfL is dynamic and is concerned with the immediate future through the daily adjustment of teaching based upon feedback. As such it requires time and energy and often involves re-conceiving the culture of the classroom, the teacher's relationship with the learner and professional dialogue with colleagues.

As indicated, AfL is not an attack on summative assessment: it is merely getting the balance right. Summative assessments are useful as they tell you (if they are reliable and valid) where you are but they do not help you improve as the information generated fails to identify the source of learning difficulty, nor does it suggest strategies for getting better. Summative assessments are a bit like going to your doctor with a pain and being told: 'It's a 6 out of 10. Next!' There is no sense of diagnosis nor guidance how to improve. The only consolation would be if the person next to you got '5 out of 10'; but then again, does 5 mean better or worse?

AfL recognizes teachers as informed professional decision makers. It is the teacher who decides the balance and timing of formative and summative assessments; it is the teacher who uses this information intelligently to inform their teaching; it is the teacher who as a consequence nurtures reflexive, resilient and autonomous learners.

The correct balance?

A simple exercise worth doing early on is to list the regular summative and formative assessments that you use on a daily basis in the style shown below. Don't skip ahead in the book – try to do this exercise early on to see what the balance is between the different forms of assessment that you use. At the end of the book you might want to revisit this list to see if your ideal balance is any different.

Figure 1.1 Summative/formative balance

Feedback that helps learning – the point of contact

Are you the kind of teacher that lights up children's faces when you walk in the classroom? Or are you the kind of teacher that when you leave the classroom – children's faces lights up!

The point of contact between assessment and learning in the classroom is through formative feedback. This means feedback that helps the learner shape and direct the next phase of learning. The key to effective feedback is through:

- causing deep thinking in the learner
- increasing reflection in the learner
- proving guidance on how to improve for the learner
- negotiating the options for the next steps for the learner.

The form of feedback can vary and can be in any direction between the teacher and the learner or the learner and another learner (peer-to-peer). The timing of the feedback should also vary, as although feedback traditionally comes at the end of a learning process this is generally too late to impact upon it. Therefore periodic or midway feedback to learners can be much more productive.

The form of the feedback might be comment-only (not grades) or verbal. Whichever form it is, it must clearly identify how to improve with an unambiguous focus being upon meeting the required criteria. Part of this feedback includes suggestions on how to improve but, importantly, not bypassing the learning process by giving complete solutions.

One potential pitfall of feedback is the creating of a learner dependency upon teachers. So, while it may be appropriate within the school for teachers to provide regular feedback to pupils, at some point the feedback has to be reduced in a managed way. For example, pupils leaving school ultimately need to have the tools to be able to reflect upon their own levels of capability and performance and decide upon the most appropriate form of action. It is unlikely that they will have a hotline to their teachers beyond their school life!

Advice

Six steps

Here are six steps for you to try in attempting to implement effective feedback as part of the AfL process. Clearly the process is adaptable and by reading through the rest of the book you will also see how each of three steps can be enhanced.

Identify the success criteria for the activity: Key outcomes and success criteria for the task should be negotiated through class discussion. This provides the learners with a sense of ownership and a clear direction on how to proceed.

Learners begin their journey: The learners start the task and continue working on it, perhaps as part of an extended activity or homework. Task and criteria should be shared with parents/carers.

Learners reflect: Peer-to-peer and self-reflective feedback against criteria identifying 3+1 (three positives and one area for improvement): teacher models 3+1 and provides feedback; teacher engages with targeted learner reflections and provides feedback.

Working on improvements: Learners spend time (deep thinking) on thinking about their identified area for improvement. Learners, with peer support and feedback, set targets for improvement.

Midway feedback: Midway through the task the teacher invests time in focusing upon learners' 3+1. Feedback is given on the learners' reflections and ways of improving the quality of reflection and target setting.

Moderation and feedback: The final stage involves feedback on the task by providing written formative feedback on how well learners have met the criteria and how effectively they have met their targets, along with setting future targets. There will be times when feedback is summative but it is important to get the correct balance.

Activity

Linking feedback to objectives

A common misconception is that teachers will often share objectives with pupils but then reward effort and industry when assessing their work. Therefore one of the most important features of AfL is clarity. This means the teacher being extremely clear about what they are teaching and the learners being absolutely clear on what they will be learning, when they will be learning it (i.e. chunks of the lesson), how this learning will be assessed and what the criteria for assessment will be.

Some of this is now very much the norm in many learning environments with the teacher, although not always convincingly, sharing the objectives at the start of the learning with the pupils. However, Ofsted reports that although many teachers will share the learning objectives at the start of the lesson, they will often resort to assessing and rewarding the more overt *behaviours* (rather than *learning*) of how hard someone appears to be working, and the quantity and neatness of work, even though these do not relate to the assessment criteria or objectives.

This is, however, only natural. Think about it – how many schools still award effort grades on school reports? As far as I know there is no single method of measuring pupils' effort that does not involve using some form of scientific calculator – yet the appearance of effort or compliance is something that we all like to comment on and reward.

AfL requires a shift in our mindset. We can still reward and recognize industry, effort and compliance elsewhere and in other ways; however, it is critical if sharing the learning with pupils that we should commit to the process and provide feedback specifically on the learning that was shared using the criteria that were identified. This 'squaring of the circle' is very much at the heart of AfL and for many teachers this represents the biggest challenge.

Advice

A simple plan to use

Pre-planning is an important part of AfL and there are many ways of doing this. However, all teachers employing AfL need to be clear about those areas identified on the grid below.

Learning Objective 1	Time to be spent on Objective 1	Criteria for assessment of Objective 1	Assessment method for Objective 1	Type of feedback for Objective 1
Learning Objective 2	Time to be spent on Objective 2	Criteria for assessment of Objective 2	Assessment method for Objective 2	Type of feedback for Objective 2
Learning Objective 3	Time to be spent on Objective 3	Criteria for assessment of Objective 3	Assessment method for Objective 3	Type of feedback for Objective 3
Learning Objective 4	Time to be spent on Objective 4	Criteria for assessment of Objective 4	Assessment method for Objective 4	Type of feedback for Objective 4

Activity

Creating the right emotional environment for feedback

Part of emotional literacy in schools (e.g. the SEAL [Promoting Social and Emotional Aspects of Learning] programme) is recognizing the vulnerability of children in the learning process. Without doubt the assessment process, and in particular negative feedback, has often been used inappropriately as a short, sharp disciplinary tool – i.e. a means of paying back a pupil.

The difficulty with feedback is that we tend to take it personally and therefore will often respond personally. For instance, during research as part of AfL it was found that children who got a low mark (summative) would often not engage with the feedback as they felt it was merely further criticism adding more anguish to the process.

In order for all children to attempt to view feedback, even though it is personal, as a positive way to improvement means removing personalities from the situation. So although some children will feel it is teachers picking on them all of the time, the reality is often different. A process of reframing is necessary to focus on what needs to change and why, rather than blanket statements of despondency. Negative or critical feedback must be viewed as providing the key to unlocking the path to improvement, while no feedback or limited feedback keeps the path locked.

One final point to remember – most of the time difficult feedback is given by someone because they care and because they are not willing to take the easy option of merely saying something palatable. Why? Because it takes much longer and is far more difficult to give what is perceived by the receiver as negative feedback.

Advice

Improving the emotional environment for feedback

Comment-only feedback (rather than marks or grades) provides a means of preventing pupils being able to easily compare themselves with each other and also provides information on how to improve.

Link feedback to learner's own self-assessment, thus focusing on the quality of the self-evaluation.

Create a trusting environment – explain why we have feedback and how it leads to improvement.

Share stories about when you have had feedback that was difficult to accept at the time but which was correct and which made you focus on improvement (if you don't have one there are plenty in the sporting world to use).

Peer-assessment often makes the feedback process more effective.

The timing of feedback is important – make sure that time is spent allowing children to engage and reflect on feedback that you have provided – early on rather than at the end of the lesson.

Make sure the assessment and feedback remain focused on the learning objectives and criteria.

Use appropriate emotive, motivating and engaging language and avoid words such as 'failed' or 'underachieved'. Be sensitive to the needs of the learner and look for opportunities to praise.

As part of developing emotional literacy it is valuable to ask and discuss with learners how they feel when they get feedback that is difficult to accept.

Look to see how your emotional literacy policy ties in with your AfL policy – they should complement each other.

Activity

Gaining feedback from learners – communication

As well as the teacher feeding back to the learner at regular intervals about their performance, an essential part of AfL (in fact all learning) is the feedback of the learner to the teacher. This can be called procedural feedback as it takes place throughout the lesson and is the means of the teacher adapting the learning journey according to need. The regular flow of information back to the teacher is central to effective learning and there are two key pieces of information that we are trying to obtain from learners which will ultimately shape how we teach. These are: first, the extent that the learners have understood the learning related to the objectives of the lesson; and second, the extent that learners understand and are able to make connections with the learning related to the bigger picture (such as where the new learning fits with a continuum of experiences). Making these connections is an essential part of learning as application contextualizes the learning more effectively.

Feedback should be gained at regular intervals throughout the lesson and can be through frequent starters and plenaries (a misconception is that these only happen at the start and end of the lesson) marking the different chunks of learning associated with the different objectives.

The two key aims of procedural feedback are: first so that diagnostic teaching can take place – therefore the teaching and, more importantly the learning, can be adjusted in real time to ensure the most effective learning is occurring; second, to have as many learners as possible engaged and challenged for the greatest amount of time during the lesson. Central to this is making the feedback process regular, familiar and accessible for the learner.

Advice

Opportunities for gaining feedback

The opportunities below are the means of getting regular feedback from learners so that teaching can be adjusted to aid the next learning phase.

Regular starters/plenaries: Interactive starters and plenaries don't just take place at the start and end of the lesson but throughout the learning – often marking each phase of learning.

Targeted questions: Pre-planned deep questions targeted at individuals or groups to ensure that all learners are challenged into providing feedback.

Think-pair-share: Whole class engaged in thinking in pairs then sharing their thinking/learning with group.

Learners assessing their own/peers' work: Learners feedback what they have had difficulty with.

Learners plan questions (with model answers) for teacher or partner: The quality of questions and answers will provide feedback on the extent of the understanding.

Self-assessment of understanding: Learners feedback on their own assessments.

Traffic lights: At the end of the lesson, learners are asked to indicate their understanding of each objective using a red, yellow or green circle, according to whether they feel they have achieved the objective fully (green), partially (yellow) or not at all (red).

Thumb-o-meter: Similar to traffic lights – thumbs up if you are confident understanding objective X, thumbs down if not.

Mini-whiteboards: For a whole range of feedback from learners relating to questions or objectives, from smiley faces to drawing, spellings, equations, etc.

Mind maps: Used by learners to tag and map their learning to make connections to other areas of learning.

Activity

Shaping the learning journey

A common question that many teachers will ask at the start of a lesson is: 'What did we learn last lesson?' It is not a bad low level, recall-type question and provides a useful reminder of what was learned. However, a much more important question to ask would be: 'Why do you think we learned what we learned last lesson and how did we learn it?'

The point is that if learning does take place in a lesson and learners think it mysteriously happened, then perhaps an opportunity has been lost. Equally if learning takes place but the learners do not understand why they were learning that piece of knowledge, new skill, or alternative concept, or developed a particular attitude towards something, then again an opportunity may have been lost. Perhaps of even more concern is if the learners (and even worse the teachers) think the learning is just so that they can pass exams.

The point of AfL is to enhance learning through increasing pupil ownership and this cannot occur in a vacuum. If learning is to be enhanced is has to be rich, based upon a continuum: a journey with multiple endings. Along this journey the learner needs to know where they are (what they understand) and more importantly where they are going and how they get there (through all forms of assessment and feedback).

If at this stage in the book you are starting to think this is all obvious – you are right. AfL is a collection of teaching strategies, many that you may already use, that can be honed as part of your teaching and learning repertoire. The key shift is that although AfL is articulated through teachers changing their practice through planning and facilitating, ultimately it is about shaping learners, developing their autonomy and increasing their ownership of the learning process.

Advice

Shaping the learning strategies –
a journey metaphor

Consider building these strategies into your journey through a lesson (when appropriate).

1. Pre-planning – identify (ideally with others) the essential stopping-off points in the journey (lesson) and plan the best route for hitting these points.

2. Share the route and learning points/objectives at start of the journey (learning) with the fellow travellers (learners).

3. Discuss/negotiate the success criteria – how will we know when we get there?

4. Map the learning – how does it build upon prior journeys (mind maps)? What other journeys have we had that we can build upon and link together?

5. What will we expect to be able to do when we get there – what are the key ingredients of a successful journey (learning outcomes)?

6. What might it all look like – 'modelling' – of exemplar locations? These modelled locations (outcomes) might include annotated examples of different standards to exemplify 'how we know when we have got there'.

7. Facilitating different routes – mix the journey (learning). We are all going the same places but we might use different strategies to get there, e.g. group work, collaborative work; travelling in different ways; loose and tight work, using posters, drama, and role play to enhance the journey so we don't get bored.

8. Identify new vocabulary that we will need to use when we get there – what are the key words that extend the success of the journey (learning)?

9. Use some big thinking questions to challenge the travellers along the way.

10. Plan feedback breaks at appropriate intervals. Mix with the travellers.

11. If anyone asks 'are we there yet?' ask them how they will know? Enjoy the view – celebrate the journey and look forward to the next one.

Activity

Differentiation – central to AfL

Central to AfL is the concept of differentiation in teaching and learning. The point being that good teaching forces differentiation and if you are teaching a class as a whole undifferentiated group, rather than planning your teaching and learning around the individual learning needs, then you cannot be teaching formatively.

Many teachers struggle with this concept and will use the term 'differentiation by outcome' as a catch-all statement to justify their lack of differentiation within their teaching. While differentiation by outcome is an option, it also requires an understanding that learners do not all have the same abilities or the same needs. They will also work in different ways and will need different levels of support and intervention to achieve an outcome. If there is genuine deep learning taking place there has to be diversity in the strategies adopted by the teacher. This comes from knowing the pupils that you teach, knowing what you are teaching, knowing what you are trying to achieve and why you are trying to achieve it.

This might all sound obvious (or not) but differentiation represents the planned and spontaneous interventions or withdrawal of teacher actions – the difficulty is choosing the right option at the right time. Differentiation, most of all, is responsive through the adjustment of the teaching process in real time according to the learning needs of the pupils – teachers are organizers of learning opportunities through adapting:

- content and context of learning
- process by which the learning is achieved
- product – the different outcomes from the learning
- classroom environment
- teacher repertoire.

Differentiation

Consider the extent to which, as part of AfL, you differentiate by attempting to complete the following, adapted from Tomlinson (2008). While attempting this, also consider how you might develop any areas you have difficulty completing.

Learning is based on diagnosis of student readiness, interest, and/or learning profile. For example, this is demonstrated in my lessons by:
Content, activities and assessments are developed in response to differing needs of various learners; for example, this is demonstrated in my lessons by:
Planned one-to-one interventions with learners are built into learning. An example of this would be:
Learners understand why they are learning and see the significance of the learning to them beyond the passing of tests. An example of this would be:
Teacher and learners work together to co-construct continual engagement and challenge for each learner. An example of this would be:
A range of methods, including whole-class learning, pairs, triads, and quads, student-selected groups, teacher-selected groups and random groups are used. An example of this in my teaching would be:
Time is used flexibly in response to learner needs. For example:
Clearly established individual and group criteria that provide guidance towards success. For example:
Learners are assessed in a variety of ways that will appropriately demonstrate their own thought and growth. An example of this in my teaching would be:

Activity

Sharing criteria

It's like knowing the teacher's secret.

Year 5 pupil definition of AfL

Central to AfL is increasing learner autonomy – the ability of the learner to be able to consciously monitor their own learning.

For this to happen in many classrooms requires a significant leap of faith, just like the first time a parent lets their child walk down the stairs on their own, or lets them leave the house alone for the first time. So even though you know it is better for them by increasing their responsibility and ownership, it is a difficult moment. The same is true in the classroom, as many teachers operate with a parental disposition and the shifting of responsibility and ownership is not easy.

Sharing the criteria with learners, however, allows them to engage in both a summative process (e.g. how have I done) by awarding themselves a grade or a mark; and a formative process (e.g. how am I doing and what do I need to do to get better) by identifying how they need to improve. Most importantly the learner is engaged in a joined-up process of cause and effect. Taking learner autonomy seriously therefore enables the teacher to allow the learners into the evaluation and grading process.

'But wait a moment', some will say 'learners are not capable of doing this – this is the teacher's job'. Or 'won't the learner be tempted to misuse this as an easy way to get good marks?' And in peer-assessment 'won't pupils just mark other pupils down if they don't like someone?'

All these thoughts are pertinent to a certain view of the learning process and certain classroom conditions. However, research has shown that in positive learning environments, learners behave responsively and supportively when encouraged to do so – in fact the research suggests that learners are often more supportive and encouraging in their comments to peers than their teachers are.

Ultimately, through sharing assessment criteria, teachers are empowering learners by allowing them to navigate their own route through the learning as well as sharing the secrets of how to recognize where they are and how they can improve.

Advice

Guidance on sharing criteria

- The teacher makes explicit reference to criteria which clearly link to the shared learning objectives.

- The criteria have to be in a language that learners understand.

- The learners have opportunities to engage in self- and peer-assessment.

- The 'modelling' of how the criteria 'can' be met is provided for learners.

- The teacher can easily recognize progress in the key concepts and skills in their subject.

- The teacher is clear about the linkage between the objectives, the outcomes and assessment criteria.

- The teacher is able to support the whole class and individual learner progress through questioning, dialogue and written feedback. This allows a more effective and diagnostic form of assessment: e.g. the learner initially identifies the source of their difficulties.

- The teacher ensures the learner understands what quality looks like and challenges misconceptions about what might or might not represent good outcomes from the learning.

Activity

Comment-only marking

It is worth reinforcing the point that comment-only marking and feedback is central to AfL. Dylan Wiliam and Paul Black (1998) – two of the key architects of AfL – emphasized that evidence from research into comment-only marking, as a means of feeding back to learners, had a profound effect upon pupils' learning. They drew upon extensive research that identified that learners paid greater attention to comments when they were not accompanied by marks. What's more, when marks were present they could have a negative effect on learner performance.

The results of the research are summarized as:

Type of feedback	Performance of the learner
Use of comment only	Improved performance sustained over the series of tasks
Use of grade and comment	Steady decline over the series of tasks
Use of grade only	Initial improvement but not sustained across the tasks

A significant effect was that high-achieving pupils maintained an elevated level of motivation irrespective of feedback type. Low-achieving pupils, when receiving 'grade-only' feedback, quickly lost interest but benefited from comment-only feedback.

Where schools had adopted comment-only feedback it had taken time to convince teachers and pupils of the benefits. However, the move to comments shifts the focus away from comparison (and disengagement of the learner) to a sharper focus on the learning.

Use the following table to examine the range and type of assessment feedback that you provide.

Advice

Comment-only checklist

	Sometimes	Regularly	Always
Comments identify what has been done well and what still needs improvement.			
Guidance on how to make improvements is provided.			
Feedback causes thinking to take place in the learner.			
Time is provided for learners to read feedback and to action plan/ target set.			
Opportunities are available for learners to clarify feedback.			
Assessment tasks are related to the criteria and shared with the learners.			
Feedback provides 'scaffold' for improvement.			
Comments on written work which address the learning needs of the individual and reflect key aspects of the subject are provided.			
Feedback is differentiated and tailored to the individual.			
Learners are encouraged to reflect on their own performance prior to comments.			
Comments are varied e.g. one-to-one, group, regular, short, long, etc.			
Comments are regular and rapid.			
Feedback develops learner autonomy.			

Activity

Planning intervention

The use of AfL transforms interventions from passive to dynamic. This means that rather than the interactions with learners being dominated by those who seek the most attention, the process becomes a much more purposeful and planned activity.

The most effective way for this is through planned intervention where the teacher deliberately plans one-to-one interventions with the learners. The basis of the intervention may be through a variety of methods such as:

- pre-planned intervention – through targeted questions in a group question and answer session.

- pre-planned intervention – through targeted question in a one-to-one session.

- pre-planned intervention – through discussion relating to target setting.

- pre-planned intervention – through discussion relating to misconceptions diagnosed as part of teacher assessment.

- pre-planned intervention – one-to-one to identify the source of difficulty.

- pre-planned intervention – to allow the learner to feed back progress related to their targets.

- pre-planned interventions – to allow learners to co-construct and negotiate their next steps in learning.

- pre-planned intervention – through providing feedback that focuses on individual improvement and progress.

- pre-planned intervention – that brings the learner into the assessment process (e.g. using criteria).

The point is that although a range of unscheduled interventions should and will always take place in a lesson, there must be opportunities for quality diagnosis and feedback to ensure all learners are regularly and individually targeted over a period of time. The active involvement of the learner in this process is crucial – so it is as much (if not more) the learner who is taking the lead in these interventions. This prevents the chances of learners slipping through the net, or learners deliberately avoiding the teacher and thus not being challenged.

Advice

Interventions planner

By identifying a number of learners (e.g. five learners) to be targeted individually, each lesson allows a whole group to be systematically and regularly targeted and monitored over a series of lessons. The targeted planning sheet therefore allows interventions to be much more formative and strategic.

Learner 1 name	Type of planned intervention (tick)	Planned intervention (e.g. question, nature of conversation, strategy)
	☐ targeted questions in a question and answer session	
Previous intervention details	☐ targeted question in a one-to-one session	
	☐ discussion relating to target setting	
	☐ discussion relating to misconceptions	
Previous targets	☐ identify the source of difficulty	
	☐ formative recording and reporting	
	☐ pupil does not understand a concept that must be revisited	
	☐ allow the learner to feedback progress and targets	
	☐ allow learner to co-construct and negotiate their next steps in learning	
	☐ feedback that focuses on individual improvement	
	☐ learner into the assessment process	

(Continued)

Activity

The use of such a system is also a re-conception of the purpose of assessment, as the assessment changes from a summative (at the end of the process) to a diagnostic and formative approach along the way.

As is often said: one definition of good teaching is when the teacher becomes progressively less visible but more effective in their interventions.

Advice

Learner 2 name	Type of planned intervention (tick)	Planned intervention (e.g. question, nature of conversation, strategy)
	☐ targeted questions in a question and answer session	
Previous intervention details	☐ targeted questions in a one-to-one session	
	☐ discussion relating to target setting	
	☐ discussion relating to misconceptions	
Previous targets	☐ identify the source of difficulty	
	☐ formative recording and reporting	
	☐ pupil does not understand a concept that must be revisited	
	☐ allow the learner to feedback progress and targets	
	☐ allow learner to co-construct and negotiate their next steps in learning	
	☐ feedback that focuses on individual improvement	
	☐ learner into the assessment process	

* Repeat as many times as necessary.

Where does all the time for this come from?

It is hoped that at this stage of the book you are already more informed, ready to read more, a little fired (not fed!) up and ready to go. But I am sure you are already saying to yourself: 'but where do I get all the time from to do this?'

It might sound paradoxical but AfL should not necessarily mean a greater need for more time – it should mean a better use of existing time. It also adheres to the 'less is more' principle in that fewer but more effective and targeted teacher interventions can be more productive than widespread blanket summative teacher assessment.

Let me explain. It has become the norm that most schools give out masses of homework and it is part of the existing school culture that this is usually all marked, turned around and returned to pupils quickly so that more homework (and therefore marking) can be done – a never-ending unquestioned cycle. For most this is a hollow whirlwind process with little time for quality feedback and reflection. It also means that the shaping of homework and assessments is geared more towards the summative rather than the formative process.

Therefore a shift is required in learning, in the school accountability culture and in parental expectations. School managers and parents have to realize the benefits of AfL and understand that it involves a shift to improving the quality of feedback to learners as well as increasing learner autonomy. This means that the learners have to take on an increased responsibility in managing their own learning so that more time may be spent on planning for learning, ensuring high level engagement and thinking rather than trying to 'catch out' who was or was not listening when it is too late.

Advice

What else needs shifting?

Shifting to AfL is only one part of the complex jigsaw of a range of school and cultural changes needed as part of a global educational challenge.

Consider whether the other areas you are involved in are also shifting.

Learning globally is moving from:	Are you shifting?	Learning globally is moving to:
Summative	Yes/no	Formative
Reactive curriculum	Yes/no	Creative curriculum
Stable learning	Yes/no	Flexible learning
Instruction	Yes/no	Co-construction
Quality controlled	Yes/no	Quality assured
Content delivery	Yes/no	User generated content
Fit into the system	Yes/no	Fit for the student
Individualized	Yes/no	Personalized
National context for learning	Yes/no	Global context for learning
Teacher-to-pupil	Yes/no	Peer-to-peer
Interactive	Yes/no	Participative
Curriculum centric	Yes/no	Learner centric
Teaching	Yes/no	Learning
Pieces of work	Yes/no	Projects of work
Piaget	Yes/no	Vygotsky
Mundane	Yes/no	Engaging

Activity

2 Questioning and dialogue

Pre-planning questions (with colleagues)

Teachers have often commented that not until they have examined their own questioning technique have they realized how poor it can actually be. Central to this are teachers prioritizing questioning in their lessons as part of AfL; not just any old questions but really good questions. In fact, for many teachers it is a reconceptualizing of the whole process of questioning. For instance, approximately 15% of classroom time is devoted to those 350 questions asked a day. However, very few are planned questions and as a result are often low level mundane questions. In fact when analysed, only around 20% of questions actually require any thinking from learners.

With AfL, however, the status of questioning is elevated to a much more significant level by conceptualizing them as central to the learning experience. Such questions need to be pre-planned and targeted to specific groups of learners to be most effective. Such pre-planning of good questions is not, however, part of our teaching culture and an often quoted example of good practice is that of Japanese teacher question planning where groups of colleagues plan questions together. The '*jugyou kenkyuu*' or 'lesson study' allows teachers to pre-plan and discuss deep probing questions designed to enhance learning. Central to this concept is that assessment is built in to the process of learning and not at the end – therefore requiring less post-learning assessment in the form of marking.

Advice

Teachers, on average, ask around 350 questions a day but many are mundane and low level. This chapter looks at how questions and dialogue can play a significant part in increasing learner engagement and understanding as part of AfL.

Engineering a different learning environment

Developing your questioning strategies demonstrates a commitment to placing learning and assessment as central features of learner progression. If you feel you need to make a gradual start to enhancing your questioning strategy, try the plan below to build up your strategies weekly.

Week 1

Use two or three big start up questions to cause thinking at the start and throughout the lesson.
Use of 'wait time' after questions.
Link questions to learning objectives.

Week 2

Basketball rather than serial table-tennis – questions are passed around the room from learner to learner rather than backwards and forwards from the teacher.
Vary question by using a variety of stems using open and closed questions.
'No hands up' strategy introduced where learners only put their hand up when asking a question – teacher involves whole class and targets learners for answers.

Activity

29

Advice

Week 3

Improved teacher questioning developed through collaborative planning of questions with colleagues.
Planned targeted questions strategy implemented.
Boy/girl alternating question strategies (if appropriate) to avoid gender bias.

Week 4

Learners plan question for teachers.
Learners plan questions for each other.
Learners plan questions to enhance own learning.

Week 5

Peer review observation (by colleague) of implementation of questioning strategies.
Traffic lights system introduced where learners feed back on level of understanding (green = fully understood, amber = partial understanding, red = not understood).
Moving from low-order (knowledge – comprehension – application) to high-order (analysis – synthesis – evaluation) questions.

Activity

Question routines

Education is more than filling a child with facts. It starts with posing difficult questions.

It is important to recognize the diverse uses of different types of question and the common pitfalls with questioning routines – get it right and you achieve a powerful learning environment.

Chewy, 'open', long and purposeful questions used for:

- finding out what a learner knows, understands and can do
- clarifying what learners have done already and what they have to do next
- fostering thinking-about-thinking (metacognition) by asking learners how and why they did what they did in the activity.

Crisp, 'closed' questions used for:

- checking recall of facts
- keeping learners focused
- a discipline tool
- increasing pace and tempo in a lesson.

Common pitfalls – when it goes wrong:

- teacher asks too many closed questions
- asking learners questions to which they can respond with a simple yes or no answer when greater elaboration is required
- asking too many short-answer, recall-based questions
- asking bogus 'guess what I'm thinking' questions
- starting all questions with the same stem
- ignoring ineffective, incorrect answers or misconceptions
- focusing on a small number of learners and not involving the whole class in thinking
- only taking volunteered answers
- making the sequence of questions too rigid and formal.

Advice

Questioning routines

Select a topic that you are teaching and see if you can use these higher level question stems to create some good AfL questions.

Analysis (The examination of the relevant information to select the best course of action)

- What was the underlying theme of ... ?
- What do you see as other possible outcomes?
- How is ... similar to ... ?
- What are some of the problems of ... ?
- Can you distinguish between ... ?
- What were some of the motives behind ... ?
- What might someone else think differently about ... ?

Synthesis (evidence and expert opinion on a specific topic to aid in decision-making)

- Can you design a ... to ... ?
- Can you see a possible solution to ... ?
- If you had access to all resources how would you deal with ... ?
- What would happen if ... ?
- How many ways can you ... ?
- Can you create new and unusual uses for ... ?
- Can you develop a proposal which would ... ?

Evaluation (Judging the value of something based upon considered personal values/opinions)

- Is there a better solution to ... ?
- Explain how X could be considered better than Y?

Activity

Effective questions:

- encourage learner engagement and participation
- build upon prior learning
- encourage independence of thought
- prevent 'faking' or 'playing the game'.

Useful question stems:

- How might we be sure that ... ?
- Can anyone explain ... ?
- How might you ... ?
- What might be another way of explaining ... ?
- How does this link to ... ?
- What does that tell us about ... ?
- What is wrong with ... ?

Advice

- Can you defend your position about . . . ?
- Do you think . . . is a good or a bad thing?
- How would you have handled . . . ?
- What changes to . . . would you recommend?
- How would you feel if . . . ?
- How effective are . . . ?
- What do you think about . . . ?

Activity

Blooming questions

'Mummy – did you and daddy really make me?'
'Yes, darling.'
'Well, how did you put my eyes in?'

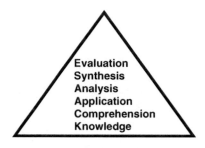

Figure 2.1 Bloom's hierarchy of learning

Asking progressively more demanding questions is central to AfL and most teachers will be familiar with the concept shown in Figure 2.1 of Bloom's hierarchy of learning. However, how can these be combined to create challenging question stems? The simplest way is to design questions based upon selecting from the different levels of challenge identified above – with the top representing the highest level and the bottom the lowest. The easiest way to do this is to select the active verb from the corresponding levels below and use these to plan questions.

Therefore if we want a low level question then learners may, for example, be asked to label (knowledge) the parts of a diagram. However, if we want a high level question then we will need to ask learners questions where they are, for example, asked to interpret (evaluate) a set of results or to estimate something based on limited information.

Question stems to use (low to high):

Knowledge: define, label, recall, order, list, quote, match, state, recognize, identify, recite

Comprehension: describe, discuss, summarize, paraphrase, report, review, understand, explain

Advice

Learners planning questions

Getting learners to plan questions for each other and for the teacher is a great way of encouraging them to work at their highest level as well as providing a real insight into their level of understanding.

Ask the learners to select from the question stems below to complete questions for each other. This will enable them to begin to develop an insight into the different levels of their own understanding.

Knowledge Low level	Can you name the . . . ? Describe what happened at . . . ? Who spoke to . . . ? Can you tell why . . . ? Can you spell . . . ? List all the . . . ? Find the meaning of . . . ? What is . . . ? Which is true or false . . . ?
Comprehension Low–mid level	Can you summarize the . . . ? What happened next after . . . ? Who were the key characters . . . ? Can you describe the . . . ? Who do you think was . . . ? What differences exist between . . . ? Can you provide a definition for . . . ?
Application	Can you think of a further example of . . . ? Can you place the following into groups . . . ? Based upon what you know what would you change if . . . ? What do you think is the key information . . . ? Can you describe for someone else how to . . . ? Would this information be useful if you had a . . . ? Where else might you use . . . ?

(Continued)

Activity

Application: assess, demonstrate, examine, distinguish, establish, show, report, implement, determine, produce, solve, draw, interpret, provide, use, utilize, write

Analysis: analyse, illustrate, discriminate, differentiate, distinguish, examine, question, infer, support, prove, test, experiment, categorize, write

Synthesis: Compile, categorize, generate, negotiate, reconstruct, reorganize, revise, validate, organize, plan, propose, set up, write, substitute, initiate, express, compare, modify, design, create, build

Evaluation: Appraise, criticize, assess, argue, justify, defend, interpret, support, estimate, evaluate, critique, review, write

Advice

Analysis	What were the main differences between . . . ?
	Can you contrast the different experiences of . . . with your own?
	Can you explain what might have happened when . . . ?
Mid level	In what ways is . . . different from . . . ?
	What are the major problems with . . . ?
	Can you explain why . . . ?
	How might we investigate . . . ?
	What were some of the motives behind . . . ?
	Can you place the following into different categories . . . ?
	Can you explain the causes of . . . ?
Synthesis	Can you design a . . . to . . . ?
	Can you create a solution to . . . ?
	Can you devise a way to . . . ?
Mid–high level	What happens if . . . ?
	How many ways can you think of . . . ?
	What are the best ways to . . . ?
	Can you develop a set of proposals which would . . . ?
Evaluation	What better solutions might there be to . . . ?
	How would you judge if X is better than Y . . . ?
	Can you defend your position about . . . ?
	Do you think . . . is a good or a bad thing?
	What might you do differently next time . . . ?
High Level	What changes are needed to improve . . . ?
	Why would you recommend . . . ?
	Why might some believe in . . . ?
	How do you feel about . . . ?
	In what ways are . . . effective . . . ?
	Why do you think about . . . ?

Activity

Using wait time

"The pause after asking a question was really difficult."
Trainee teacher trying to implement wait time in her lesson.

I once went to a seminar on silence. I didn't purposefully go, I rather accidentally stumbled upon it as it wasn't the type of seminar I would normally sign up to. It was, however, fascinating as it was about nothing. Nothing in the sense it was about silence and the presenter used silence to great effect by using long pauses to promote thinking. At first it felt quite uncomfortable but once we got used to it, it was surprising how quickly the group used the thinking time productively.

Most teachers will be familiar with the concept of wait time – that teachers on average wait less than one second between asking a question and intervening with a learner. It is worth understanding, however, that 'wait time' can be interpreted and used in more than one way. For instance, it is recognized that the effect of the teacher creating a wait time (approximately 3–5 seconds) before taking an answer has a significant impact upon increasing learning as the number of learners engaged in thinking hopefully increases as well as the quality of the answer improving. However, a second wait time can also occur when the teacher finally offers to take a response (targeted response). There should equally follow a further wait time before the teacher (or another learner) acknowledges how correct the answer may be – so that learner can extend, question or elaborate on their answer.

It is, however, important that the wait time is not the only strategy and that strong, high level questions are also used when adopting the wait time strategy.

Advice

Peer observation – using wait time strategy

The simple proforma below can be used as part of peer observation to monitor the use of wait times as part of peer observation. The observation by a colleague should be planned for a short section of teaching and questioning (about 15 minutes) and can be used as the basis of a discussion about the effectiveness of the wait time questioning strategy.

Question and question number	Teacher question level – Bloom's hierarchy	Wait time by teacher in seconds	Wait time by teacher in response to learner answer	Additional information e.g. use of targeted question, think-pair-share, etc.
e.g. 1 What happens if you mix oil and water?	Knowledge Comprehension Application Analysis (Synthesis) Evaluation	1 2 3 (4) 5 6 7 8 9 10 11 12 Other –	1 (2 3) 4 5 6 7 8 9 10 11 12 Other –	Pupil shouted out answer even though you asked pupils not to call out – might consider bigger signal about no calling out
	Knowledge Comprehension Application Analysis Synthesis Evaluation	1 2 3 4 5 6 7 8 9 10 11 12 Other –	1 2 3 4 5 6 7 8 9 10 11 12 Other –	
	Knowledge Comprehension Application Analysis Synthesis Evaluation	1 2 3 4 5 6 7 8 9 10 11 12 Other –	1 2 3 4 5 6 7 8 9 10 11 12 Other –	
	Knowledge Comprehension Application Analysis Synthesis Evaluation	1 2 3 4 5 6 7 8 9 10 11 12 Other –	1 2 3 4 5 6 7 8 9 10 11 12 Other –	

(Continued)

Activity

Advice

42

	Knowledge Comprehension Application Analysis Synthesis Evaluation	1 2 3 4 5 6 7 8 9 10 11 12 Other –	1 2 3 4 5 6 7 8 9 10 11 12 Other –	
	Knowledge Comprehension Application Analysis Synthesis Evaluation	1 2 3 4 5 6 7 8 9 10 11 12 Other –	1 2 3 4 5 6 7 8 9 10 11 12 Other –	
	Knowledge Comprehension Application Analysis Synthesis Evaluation	1 2 3 4 5 6 7 8 9 10 11 12 Other –	1 2 3 4 5 6 7 8 9 10 11 12 Other –	

Activity

Involving everyone in dialogue

Thought = social talk made internal
Writing = internal thought/social talk made external

Language shapes and clarifies our thoughts and helps us frame concepts as well as opening up and sharing our ideas so that they can be challenged. Given that talk is so important, it is interesting how little time is spent encouraging dialogue in many schools and that old-fashioned views still permeate the profession. For example, I once visited a school and the headteacher was giving me a tour. As we were passing the classrooms where lessons were taking place he stopped, smiled and cupped his hand around his ear. 'Listen,' he said. 'I can't hear anything,' I replied. 'Exactly – silence; isn't it brilliant? We have some wonderful teachers here'.

The art of getting a class full of pupils silent is a skill most teachers would admire. However, the headteacher had missed the point and had placed control of the pupils higher than their learning. Learning cannot take place in a vacuum and it is at its best when there is a rich two-way dialogue between teacher and learner and learner and learner.

In terms of teaching it is important that we value learner dialogue but also recognize that in order to enhance speaking and listening we need to provide learners with a set of tools so that they recognize the different forms of talk and match these to the correct occasion. It is therefore essential that teachers model, shape and clarify dialogue as a central part of learning as well as recognizing dialogue as a central feature of assessment.

The way that learners talk with each other determines the way they will think and the way they will write.

Advice

Speaking and listening groups

The purpose of this exercise is to promote active listening while also developing high level evaluative and synthesis thinking skills.

1. Split a class into groups of four to discuss a particular aspect of the lesson – perhaps related to a big question.

2. The group discusses key aspects of the topic and comes up with their outcomes e.g. an answer to the question.

3. One person from each group takes a turn to visit another group for a set time where they will discuss their answer to the big question. The corresponding person from another group also moves around so that there are always four in each group. Notes are allowed to be taken and when they each return to their original group (after visiting a set number of groups) their original answer is adapted and developed based upon their discussions.

4. An agreed answer is then presented by each group to the teacher who then discusses similarities, differences, etc.

Activity

Targeting questions

Hope is not a strategy...

Have you ever seen the film *Sixth Sense*, where the child can see dead people? Well, I sometimes sit observing lessons and occasionally feel as if I can see the ghost children.

These are the children that ghost in, on and through a lesson without ever being seen. It's a mutual trade-off. The teacher knows they are there but won't make too many demands upon them as long as they don't make too much fuss.

The reality is that in any class 80% of your time is often taken up by a 20% minority of either very bright or very naughty (or a combination of both) pupils. The ghost children are the ones in the middle, those whose name you can never quite remember and that you hope are getting on okay. They are right in the middle – they are not the brightest or the most demanding. They just get on but ultimately seem to be getting a raw deal. However, the ghost children, as with all learners, need to be challenged and engaged too.

The key to this is moving away from hope as a strategy and moving towards a more systematic way of intervening with all learners, including your ghost children; this is easy to do through targeting all learners in a group. This means systematically recording (using the following example) intended interventions prior to a lesson, e.g. planned questions for individuals and methods for creating opportunities for discussion with all pupils on a one-to-one basis over a set period of time.

By also regularly reviewing and identifying where learners are in their learning curve, such as those who are coasting, again helps when prioritizing who is targeted and how.

Advice

Targeted intervention

The template below can be adapted to be used both as a register and also a means of systematically recording details of the planned interventions with all learners over a series of weeks; for example, one planned intervention may be pre-planned questions for an individual. Identifying those learners working at low level, coasting (ghost learners) or exceeding the objectives allows different actions to be taken with individual learners through planned intervention.

Learner name	Planned intervention	Learners working below objectives:
		Action:
		Learners who are coasting with objectives:
		Action:
		Learners who are exceeding objectives:
		Action:

Activity

Think-pair-share

John Holt, in his seminal book *How Children Fail* (1995), identified a whole range of strategies that children employ to avoid learning as well as a whole range of strategies that teachers and pupils employ to avoid the difficulties associated with learning. You will therefore no doubt begin to see a link: the recurring theme in this book is all about extending opportunities for increasing learning through reflection and thinking as a means of securing understanding for all learners.

In the traditional classroom, however, the teacher has conventionally engaged with one pupil at a time while the rest of the group give the impression of being engaged (or don't pretend at all).

The simple strategy of 'think-pair-share' restructures this arrangement by engaging the whole class in thinking, speaking and listening through getting pupils to share and clarify their thinking with their partners. The process starts with a big question followed by 'wait time' followed by discussion and sharing through cooperative learning with peers. This releases the teacher to be more effective through planned strategic intervention with small groups of individuals rather than reactive with dominant individuals.

Central to think-pair-share is the concept of PIES:

Positive interdependence (a structured activity that requires a group to complete a task)

Individual accountability (Individual contribution with the task is also identifiable and accountable)

Equal participation (everyone contributes and takes turns)

Simultaneous interaction (all participants are active – if not speaking then listening, etc.)

Advice

Think-pair-share

The possibilities for think-pair-share are only limited by the teacher's imagination and can be used for a whole range of strategies to enhance learning. This includes strategies such as cascading, triads, snowballing, pairs to fours, etc. The template below can easily be adapted to accommodate different ideas and can be used at any time for example:

- as part of a starter activity based upon prior knowledge
- at any stage to check understanding of material
- at the end of a teaching episode to identify the next stage of learning
- to deal with complex or difficult topics as a means of identifying difficulties
- at regular intervals to chunk up a lesson and to consolidate the learning
- as part of a plenary session.

Think-Pair-Share/One to Pairs to Fours

Names:

What I/we have been asked to think about

Think: My thoughts	Pair-Share: Our thoughts	Pairs to Fours: Our thoughts

Our collective response

Activity

Look, no hands

One of the dangers with AfL is that it becomes a series of strategies which work towards AfL but collectively do not achieve AfL. The sum of the parts does not create the whole. So while the 'no hands' strategy is now increasingly part of the classroom repertoire, unless it is integrated with the other strategies and the overall aims of AfL it will have limited impact.

The point of 'no hands' is, however, a good one. Do you remember being at school and trying to be the one selected to give an answer to the teacher's question by putting your arm high into the air while trying to remain seated, stretching every sinew just so you could get your arm an inch higher than the person in front? Did you ever look around at some of the other pupils who might not be trying so hard? Or perhaps you were the one who sat back knowing the teacher would pick one of those pupils whose seams on the armpits of their jumpers were about to rip due to the forces being exerted from the desperate extension of their arms.

The use of the 'no hands' strategy is ultimately a move away from random participation in the lesson where pupils put their hands in the air offering to answer a question while others sit back comfortably knowing they won't be selected. The 'no hands' rule creates a climate where everyone is encouraged to participate and where everyone is expected to be able to contribute to the answer in some way. Part of this comes from the teacher having planned some really challenging questions and part from creating a wait time (including think-pair-share and targeted questions) to allow all learners to consider how they may be able to contribute to the answer. So although all learners might not get the right answer, often answers revealing a misunderstanding provide good feedback for the teacher, enabling correction of any misconceptions.

Advice

Is it working?

All of the strategies in this book are to enhance learning. Here are some further ways to find out if the teaching has been successful.

One-minute summary: Learners have one minute at the end of the lesson (or at any stage) to write a summary of their learning in that lesson. Teacher uses it to see if the learners have grasped the key concepts.

One-minute mud: Learners have one minute to write down anything they didn't understand (muddy concepts).These are handed back to the teacher at the end of the lesson and are used to plan the basis of the next lesson.

One-student summary: At key points (every 15 minutes) in the lesson, one learner is asked to summarize in 30 seconds the learning so far for the rest of the group.

Learning logs: Learners maintain a learning log which identifies what they have learned and what they need to learn. This is simply a page divided into two and subdivided by weeks.

Which was best? Instead of asking whether the objectives of the lesson were met (to which lazy learners might simply say yes), the teacher asks in which ways did we meet the objectives and which objectives were the most and least successful.

Plan questions for other classes: One class, based upon their own learning, plans difficult questions for parallel classes who may be working on the same topic.

Post-it: Teacher draws the shape below on a whiteboard or poster and learners complete Post-it notes and stick them in the appropriate box as a means of feedback.

What I understand:	What I would like more of:

Key questions to frame the learning

Assessment is like a double-edged sword. It may be turned to dangerous uses if it is not properly handled.

I sometimes see teachers introduce the objectives to a lesson in a very unenthusiastic, almost apologetic (I've been told I have to do this) way. It is clear that they are not convinced of the worth of such an activity and the learners soon get the picture that this is something the teacher is forced to do.

An alternative to having objectives in a lesson is to frame the lesson in terms of questions that the learners will not be able to answer at the start but will be able to answer by the end of the lesson as a result of the learning that is about to take place.

The point with this is that instead of sharing what will be learned in the form of the learning objectives, the learning is shared in terms of big questions that will frame the lesson. Therefore the sharing of the learning will include: 'In today's lesson we are going to focus on three big questions, which at the moment you won't be able to answer but you will by the end of today's lesson.'

By doing this identifies both the outcomes of the learning as well as the assessment that will be taking place. Also, by using this method, there is also the opportunity to recognize the different achievements by learners when responding to the questions.

Using questions to frame the lesson also secures the plenary as there is a clear focus on the extent to which all learners were able to answer the questions set at the start. Central to all of this is the teacher's commitment to learning, along with comprehensive preparation of high level 'wicked' questions to provoke thinking and encourage dialogue.

Advice

Climbing Blooming Mountain

Climbing Blooming Mountain can be completed in a variety of ways such as the teacher planning progressively more difficult questions week by week (starting at week one with low level knowledge); or learners planning more difficult questions for their peers each week; or finally the learners planning more difficult questions for their teacher each week or any combination of the above.

However, over the six-week activity the higher level questions and number of questions increase. Ideally this can be fun and drawn out on a large sheet of paper for completion to show progression.

	Ground level	Camp 1	Camp 2	Camp 3	Camp 4	The summit
						Evaluation Question:
					Synthesis Question:	Synthesis Question:
				Analysis Question:	Analysis Question:	Analysis Question:
			Application Question:	Application Question:	Application Question:	Application Question:
		Comprehension Question:	Comprehension Question:	Comprehension Question:	Comprehension Question:	Comprehension Question:
	Knowledge Question:	Knowledge Question:	Knowledge Question:	Knowledge Question:	Knowledge Question:	Knowledge Question:

Activity

Socratic questioning

Socrates, who lived over 2000 years ago, was perhaps a natural user of AfL as he believed in *ex duco*, meaning to draw or lead out learning from the student. Central to this were questioning and dialogue. This stratagem obviously worked as both Plato and Aristotle were his students and they seemed to go on to make names for themselves (we won't mention what happened to Socrates).

The aim of Socratic questioning is to challenge accuracy and completeness of thinking in a way that acts to move the learner towards achieving some form of deeper understanding. This is achieved through different stages of questioning, as outlined below, with each stage probing a different facet of understanding and thinking. This is further extended through the probing at each stage by extending the search for evidence, reason and justification. So while the learner may have some evidence – is it good evidence?

Conceptual clarification questions: Getting the learner to think about what they are thinking. This involves simple 'tell me more' questions that get the learner to externalize and explain their deeper thinking.

Probing assumptions: This makes the learner think about the assumptions and unchallenged beliefs on which they may be basing their argument and understanding. This is very much about the learner providing evidence to back up their thinking.

Questioning viewpoints and perspectives: This stage looks at the particular angle that the learner is looking from. This challenges a particular position by examining if there are other, equally valid, viewpoints.

Probe implications and consequences: This extends the challenge by asking whether their thinking can form a general rule that can be applied elsewhere and what are the pitfalls if such assumptions are applied in a detrimental way. This checks the robustness of thinking through a set of probing questions.

Questions about the question: This stage questions whether the answers to the question have really answered the question by turning the question in on itself.

Advice

Socratic question structure

Socratic questions	Planned questions

1. Questions that seek clarification:

   Can you explain that . . . ? Explaining

   What do you mean by . . . ? Defining

   Can you give me an example . . . ? Giving examples

   How does that help . . . ? Supporting

   Does anyone have a question to ask . . . ?

2. Questions that probe, reason and evidence:

   Why do you think that . . . ? Forming an argument

   How do we know that . . . ? Assumptions

   What are your reasons . . . ? Reason

   Do you have evidence . . . ? Evidence

   Can you give me an example/counter example . . . ?

3. Questions that explore alternative views:

   Can you put it another way . . . ? Re-stating views

   Is there another point of view . . . ? Speculation

   What if someone were to suggest that . . . ? Alternative views

   What would someone who disagreed with you say . . . ? Counter argument

   What is the difference between those views/ideas . . . ?

4. Questions that test implications and consequences:

   - What follows (or can we work out from) what you say . . . ? Implications
   - Does it agree with what was said earlier . . . ? Consistency
   - What would be the consequences of that . . . ? Consequences
   - Is there a general rule for that . . . ? Generalizing rules – How could you test to see if it was true . . . ?

(Continued)

Activity

Advice

Socratic questions	Planned questions

5. Questions about the question/discussion:

- Do you have a question about that . . . ? Questioning
- What kind of question is it . . . ? Analysing
- How does what was said/the question help us . . . ? Connecting
- Where have we got to – who can summarize so far . . . ? Summarizing
- Are we any closer to answering the question/solving the problem . . . ?

Putting it all together

If you're not learning then I am just talking.

This section has focused very much upon questioning strategies as part of AfL. Absolutely critical is that this process is considered as a closed loop: that is, the assessments through questions inform the subsequent learning, planning and teaching. This means that:

The teacher evolves from mere presentation of facts to exploration of learner's ideas, involving the learner in the journey.

The learner's role evolves to become more active, realizing that learning depends on engagement and readiness to express and discuss and not on spotting or guessing the right answers.

The teacher spends more effort on planning and framing questions to explore issues critical to the development of the learner's understanding.

An important point is that most teachers will not recognize AfL from their own learning experiences and no matter how long you have been teaching, moving to AfL will involve some uncertainty as you unpick your teaching practices. Such a journey is both an emotional (dealing with risk and uncertainty) and professional one. Such a journey also dramatically re-conceives the assessment process from being one of telling the learner where they are to empowering the learner to be able to self-identify where they are, to know where they are going and how they can get there.

Advice

Observation

This proforma below is designed to aid peer observation of teaching and learning based upon some of the essential principles of the Key Stage 3 strategy – central to this is a strong emphasis on questioning and AfL principles.

Lesson Time:

Year Group:

Lesson Context:

Starter activity or Introduction:

Questioning strategies:

	Yes	No	Frequency
Targeted Q			
Random Q			
Open Q			
Closed Q			
Stepped Q			
Procedural Q			
Question wait time			
Plenaries			

	Yes	No
Starter built upon	☐	☐
Pace	☐	☐
Explain Language	☐	☐
Links to literacy	☐	☐
Links to numeracy	☐	☐

	Yes	No
Task explicit	☐	☐
Shared criteria	☐	☐
Exemplar material	☐	☐
Individual formative feedback	☐	☐
Teacher observation	☐	☐
Individual targets set	☐	☐
Self assessment	☐	☐
Peer assessment	☐	☐

Activity

3

Further elements of AfL and learning

The learner and assessment – peer-assessment

Peer-to-peer discussion and assessment plays an essential part in creating a positive learning environment where assessment is central to the learning. However to many learners the concept will be alien and many times I have seen and heard pupils trying to get to grips with the idea:

> 'Yer mean, you want me to mark her work for you!'
> or
> 'I'm not showing him my work!'

It is therefore important that learners are carefully introduced to the concept of peer-assessment as well as being given the tools to carry it out effectively.

Structuring the peer-to-peer conversations, for example, using oral frames, is a really useful way of ensuring the peer-assessment exercise is a positive experience. Creating the right emotional and motivational environment is also important and this is best achieved through modelling the peer-assessment process.

Ultimately peer-assessment engages the whole class in high level thinking through ownership of the assessment process. This provides valuable information for the learner as well as identifying important real time information for the addressing of misconceptions through adjusting of the teaching.

Advice

AfL is more than a set of strategies – it is having a clear approach to learning and therefore involves a multitude of factors. This chapter extends our understanding by considering further elements to be considered when implementing AfL.

Structuring and supporting peer discussion

- Sample guidance to be adapted, elaborated and then shared with learners prior to peer-assessment exercise.
- We learn from discussion with one another.
- Discussing the assessment of one another's work helps us understand how to get better.
- It is important to look for both strengths and areas that can be improved.
- Although we might not like hearing what needs to be improved – this is the best type of feedback.
- Don't be surprised if you feel uncomfortable getting told what needs to improve. No one likes bad feedback but in the end we know it is good (perhaps give a personal example).
- When assessing your partner's work it is important that you discuss it against the criteria – don't just focus upon how much work has been done or how neat the work is.
- All students must contribute; that way everyone gets better.
- If you are working with a friend and want to be a good friend then honesty is essential when giving feedback.
- When working in groups everyone should participate and no one member should say too much or too little.
- Every contribution must be treated with respect and listened to thoughtfully.
- If you don't agree then you must work towards a consensus to resolve your differences.
- Every suggestion for improvement has to be justified – all arguments must include reasons.
- We use the 'two stars and a wish' approach so find two positives and one area for improvement.

Activity

Engaging learners with criteria

Sometimes when I try harder and harder, I just get worser and worser.

James, year 7

Throughout this book there has been a consistent message related to AfL, which is to engage learners in the criteria for assessment. For many teachers this will be quite an abstract idea as often the criteria are something of a 'secret garden'. However, there are three clear ways that this can be achieved:

Learners create and define their own criteria: This is achieved through the learners setting their own success criteria or group success criteria. This does not mean that the teacher is completely passive in this role but it does mean that the learners have a degree of autonomy through ownership in the identification of potential success criteria and levels of performance required for illustrating increased attainment.

Learners exemplify existing criteria: This is when learners take existing criteria (e.g. from an exam board) and translate them into accessible learner language as well as suggesting what the exemplification of the criteria may look like. The exemplification is based upon putting prior learning into action as well as identifying what else might need to be learned to more successfully meet the criteria.

Learners negotiate criteria weights: This is when the teacher has identified the criteria but the learner can negotiate which aspects of the criteria they wish to focus upon. This is particularly useful in extended projects where the weightings of the assessment can be negotiated so that the learners are focusing on particular aspects of their work.

The ultimate aim of engaging learners in assessment is that they realize and understand how they are being assessed and that they develop a clear understanding of the learning associated with the criteria. This removes the mystique of assessment – something that is done to them – and opens up assessment and learning as something which they personally own.

Advice

Criteria alert sheet

A good strategy is for learners to have an ongoing criteria alert sheet which can be used for individual subjects or across all subjects. Either way it is simply a means of removing the guesswork of what is required.

⚠	**Criteria Alert**	⚠
Task	Criteria	Good work might include
1		
2		
3		
4		
5		

From quality control to quality assurance

I once visited an aircraft engine factory and when speaking to one of the staff I rhetorically suggested that they must have a really good quality control system. He replied that there was no quality control process at the factory as what tended to happen was that people got casual in their work because they knew there was a safety net at the end – which you wouldn't want when building aircraft engines! Therefore they employed really good quality assurance procedures – quality was built into each stage of the process rather than a final check at the end.

In many ways AfL embodies this way of thinking. Instead of waiting until the end of the process and ensuring through quality control (e.g. a test or marked piece of work) that everything is okay, quality assurance procedures are put in place and action is taken in real time.

Such an approach recognizes and increases learning responsibility and autonomy – essential to lifelong learning and ownership of the learning – by removing the safety net that many learners become dependent upon.

Building quality assurance into AfL is only one part of a continuum of activities that contribute to the development of teaching and learning. This can be done in many effective ways including using learner voice (expert witness), peer observation, coaching and continued professional development. For example, learners may be asked what aspects of AfL they find unhelpful or beneficial.

The implementation of AfL can also be quality assured through peer observation, with the analysis of learner voice and peer observation feeding into professional development and coaching systems.

Advice

Building in quality assurance

Quality assurance is now central to School Self-Evaluation and this procedure identifies the steps and evidence for building in aspects of AfL. The steps are about assuring the quality of learning while it is happening and providing real time data to inform teaching and learning as well as evidence for the self-evaluation process.

- Theme discussed and developed from a departmental meeting (evidence provided through agenda and minutes). This could be, for example, to focus on the quality of questioning in lessons.

- The follow-up meeting would generate discussion, perhaps based upon the literature on questioning that would be presented at the meeting (further evidence).

- An agreed schedule may be drawn up for teachers to observe each other (more evidence) with a proforma for recording the nature, type and frequency of questioning being developed (further evidence). Peer observations generate additional evidence which would then be used to generate discussion at the next meeting followed by further observations and discussion (all generating extra evidence).

- Learner's feedback gathered and discussed (further evidence). Teaching amended/fine tuned upon the basis of the analysis of evidence.

- Ultimately this activity would naturally be generating evidence as well as improving the quality of teaching and learning through the improved questioning technique of teachers and feedback from learners. The data provided from agendas, minutes, proformas and observations would also provide excellent quality assurance evidence.

Activity

Lesson design – building in not adding on

For many teachers AfL has come along at a time when they are already established in their careers and when a seemingly successful teaching repertoire has already been established. As such many successful teachers have tried to integrate AfL into their existing routine with varying degrees of success.

What many teachers have found, however, is that although they have tried to build in AfL it has proved difficult within their existing teaching routines. A common feature has been that while teachers could tell a learner what was correct or incorrect, they couldn't always clearly explain within a task how to improve or be able to identify the source of the difficulty. This was not because the teachers lacked knowledge – it was the fact that the existing structures and tasks were too closed and did not lead to genuine learning opportunities where teachers could offer advice on how to improve or, more importantly, provide opportunities for learners to identify the best way to improve.

Central to this and AfL is the design of lessons. Notice the difference in terminology between the 'planning' of a lesson and 'design' of a lesson. The former suggests one route in establishing a lesson while the latter suggests a multitude of routes providing a range of options to choose from.

Designing a good lesson or learning experience requires good subject knowledge, an understanding of how learners do or do not learn and what concepts, skills, attitudes and knowledge create difficulties when learning.

Ultimately the aim is to design rich collaborative learning environments that focus on the learner's incremental improvement as co-constructors of their learning and where AfL is embedded into rather than added onto the learning experience.

Advice

Lesson design

You will have seen a planning proforma similar to this before; however, there are a few differences here. The first is that learning takes priority over teaching – so there is more space for writing what and how. Second, the lesson is to be planned in chunks related to each objective. Third, there are mini-plenaries at the end of each chunk of learning. Ultimately teachers need to design (not plan) their best route to learning.

Finally it is important that the learning is identified first – followed by the best type of teaching to achieve this (and not the other way around).

Episode	Learning What/How	Teaching What/How	Outcome/Assess What/How
Intro/Starter			
Objective 1 Plenary			
Objective 2 Plenary			
Objective 3 Plenary			
Plenary			

Activity

Writing objectives

I have one objective – to get to the end . . .

There are so many views about objectives that I could write an entire (and probably very boring) book about them. There are also so many chapters in books about the different types of objective that ultimately it can all be a bit confusing. Most teachers will not have thought much about objectives since they were training to be a teacher, yet the sharing and clarifying of objectives with the learner is central to AfL.

So what are 'learning objectives'? In my view a learning objective is simply what skills, attitudes, concepts or knowledge the teacher intends the learners to learn. They can also be referred to as the 'learning goals' of the lesson or the 'learning intentions'. Classifying the learning objective as a skill, attitude, concept or knowledge is, however, important as it means the delivery, learning and assessment of that learning will differ based upon its type.

For every learning objective there must also be a corresponding learning outcome as the outcomes demonstrate learners' achievements.

When writing a learning objective – simply to get you in the mindset of learning and not just focusing on the 'doing' or the 'task' – I suggest you always start with: Pupils will learn . . .

When writing an accompanying learning outcome, again to get you in the mindset of considering the form of outcome, I would suggest that you always start with: Pupils will be able to . . . – followed by an active verb based upon Bloom's hierarchy of learning – e.g. list, describe, analyse, evaluate, etc.

The objectives that the teacher writes in their 'lesson design' may, however, not be exactly the same as those they share with their class. It may be that the teacher converts the objectives into 'pupil speak' or the teacher may simply share the outcomes and assessment or may share the questions that the learners will be able to answer at the end of the lesson. Whichever method is chosen it is critical that teachers engage with this process and consider how this is best shared with the learners.

Advice

Objective planner

This template focuses on two areas:

- The type of learning.
- The outcomes (and level of) as a result of the learning.

Learning objective – based upon: Skills (S), Attitudes (A), Concepts (C), Knowledge (K). **Outcome** – level based upon: Knowledge, comprehension, application, analysis, synthesis, evaluation.	S	A	C	K
e.g. Obj. Pupils will learn: How images can be manipulated in Photoshop				✓
e.g. Out. Pupils will be able to: *describe* five image manipulation tools.				
Obj.1 Pupils will learn:				
Out.1 Pupils will be able to:				
Obj.2 Pupils will learn:				
Out.2 Pupils will be able to:				
Obj.3 Pupils will learn:				
Out.3 Pupils will be able to:				
Obj.4 Pupils will learn:				
Out.4 Pupils will be able to:				

Activity

Sharing Objectives using WILF, WALT and OLI

Most teachers will by now be familiar with WILF (What I'm Looking For), WALT (We Are Learning Too) and OLI (Our Learning Intention is). There has, however, increasingly been some criticism of these strategies. This is because although they were a useful means of getting AfL strategy going when sharing the learning was not necessarily part of the teaching culture, they are now ultimately recognized as limited. For example WILF, although in essence a good idea, has tended to be used to give the children the success criteria and tightly constrain the learning instead of engaging children in generating what might be worth looking for.

Fundamental to AfL is that learners have a clear understanding of what they are trying to learn (learning objectives), how they can recognize achievement (learning outcomes), what 'good' looks like (success criteria) and why they are learning this material in the first place (the big picture). This is the base level.

How each of these are arrived at can be considered the second tier – for example, getting learners involved in identifying the assessment, criteria and objectives.

The third tier probably represents the real entry into AfL as this is where objectives, outcomes and assessment come together in real time to influence teaching, where learners are active in the learning process and where their ownership and responsibility increases.

Moving through these levels is, however, difficult and requires more than a change in teaching – it requires a whole-school change in culture which involves all teachers and parents understanding the key principles of AfL.

Advice

Learner personal reflection

This layout can be adapted and used to frame and promote learner reflection. It should be used sparingly but is a good means of supporting personal learner reflection.

- Today we were learning about:
- The best part of the lesson was:
- The most interesting part of the lesson was:
- The hardest part of the lesson was:
- The most important thing I learned was:
- The best thing I said was:
- I thought that _____ made the best contribution to the lesson because:
- If I could do this lesson again the one thing I would change is:
- One thing I would like to have learned more about in the lesson was:
- I must ask my teacher:
- I must find out for myself:
- My two stars and a wish are:

Activity

Model and share

Central to AfL is the sharing and modelling of good practice. This is an attempt to remove the mystique associated with assessment and place learning and understanding central to good teaching.

This can operate at several levels and includes:

- Teachers modelling and sharing good practice with each other through peer review and coaching, for example, a teacher demonstrates to another teacher their implementation of an AfL strategy such as think – pair – share, Socratic questioning, etc.

- Teachers modelling and sharing good practice through demonstrating to learners their own ability, for example, a teacher thinks aloud while doing a problem solving exercise on the whiteboard and explains to and shares with the learners the difficulties encountered.

- Teachers asking learners to decide whether they think an answer is reasonable, whether they can add to the answer, or whether they would have given another answer.

- Teachers modelling and sharing good practice from pupils, for example, the teacher shows a model answer for a piece of homework and explains why it meets the criteria and how it could be improved.

- Learners modelling and sharing good practice with each other, for example, a learner explains how they attempted a piece of work and how they have met the criteria.

- Learners using the success criteria to comment on strengths and weaknesses of each other's work and to identify areas for improvement.

- Teachers asking a question in a lesson, taking the answer and then rephrasing the answer into a model answer.

- Teachers using examples of work from anonymous students and asking their peers to suggest possible improvements and how the learning criteria could have been met more effectively.

Advice

Project evaluation

This project proforma can be used as part of a continuum of learning to get the learner to feed back on previous targets and set new targets.

Project Title:				
Name:		Group:		
My three previous main targets from my last project were: 1. 2. 3.				
In this project I have:	Not at all	A little	Well	Really well
Met target 1:				
Met target 2:				
Met target 3:				
I have met the project criteria in the following ways:				
My three new targets in priority order are: 1. 2. 3.				
Based upon the criteria I am working at Grade/Level:				
To progress to the next level I think I need to: 1. 2. 3.				

AfL and personalized learning

Effective teachers are continually updating what they know about each child's progress and using the information to plan next steps with precision.

The Children's Plan (DfCSF, 2008)

In the bad old days, schools were uniform in that they taught and assessed using the same materials for all learners in the same way. As a result, certain types of learners were successful and then went on to replicate the system based on an 'it never did me any harm' mentality.

Then came personalization and increasingly 'personalized learning' which, although an expedient political term searching for a meaning, offers an alternative way of conceiving the diversity of learning approaches. Those that have been charged while searching for a meaning for 'personalized learning' have, however, firmly placed AfL – particularly dialogic talk – as one of the key gateways within the personal learning agenda.

Ultimately AfL is central to the concept of personalization and essential to this is that every child knows how they are doing and understands what they need to do to improve and how to get there. Part of this is through increasing learner autonomy and ownership of the learning and assessment process, created through strong emotional and motivational support, often best delivered at a personal level.

This can be achieved through a clear repertoire of interactions designed to:

- praise or build confidence in individuals
- pose questions to individuals based upon extending their learning
- correct an error based upon a misconception or misunderstanding
- establish a dialogue in developing relationships to increase emotional support and motivation
- challenge and extend individual thinking towards an 'ambitious trajectory of improvement'
- clarify thinking or suggest a new approach based upon a personal knowledge of the learner.

The longevity of the term 'personalization' is questionable; however, the most robust feature of it appears to be the AfL principles embedded within this book.

Advice

AfL and personalized learning – dialogic talk

Use the checklist to see if dialogic talk is part of your personalized AfL approach.

Personalized dialogic approaches related to AfL	Yes/No
Teacher's questions are structured to provoke thoughtful answers and reflection. Pupils' answers provoke further questions and dialogue.	
Learners are encouraged to ask questions and provide explanations for each other.	
Teacher uses one-to-one monitoring with pupils which is long enough to make a difference. The dialogue is formative rather than supervisory and provides clear feedback on which the learner can build.	
Learners who are not engaged in speaking actively participate through active listening, looking, reflecting and evaluating.	
The learning environment is designed to encourage participation and dialogic teaching and learning.	
A reciprocal environment is encouraged where teachers and learners listen to each other, share ideas and consider alternative viewpoints.	
The emotional environment is important and learners have the confidence to take risks, make mistakes, and deal with uncertainty.	
Questioning builds upon prior knowledge and elicits evidence of learners' understanding. Questions prompt a range of responses including closed, narrow, open, discursive and speculative – rather than invitations to guess the one 'right' answer.	
Learners understand that talk does not always just happen and that structured responses are often needed in different contexts of talk. Learners understand those differences and can use narratives, explanation, instruction and negotiation.	

Activity

Learner (pupil) voice

Often associated with 'learner voice' is the term 'expert witness' which recognizes that children are very well placed to give teachers feedback about the learning and assessment processes within the classroom. Learners can provide rich and penetrating evidence and insight into what works well in lessons and what does not. Engaging learners in school self-evaluation also helps them develop as reflective learners and practitioners in much the same way as it helps teachers.

For many teachers, however, this goes against the grain of the way most adults were brought up which was to be 'seen but not heard' and many teachers feel vulnerable at the thought of pupils giving the 'low down' on their teachers. For some teachers there may even be a feeling of resentment as asking pupils their opinion gives them the appearance of an elevated status creating a them-vs-us scenario.

However, there is a significant misconception about learner's voice and that is that just because a pupil says something does not make it correct; what it does is provide a rich insight into pupils' perceptions which can provide incredibly valuable information about their beliefs and misconceptions.

In essence it provides a shortcut to finding out quickly what otherwise may go unnoticed. Intrinsic to this is the concept of partners in learning, as ultimately learners and teachers want the same outcomes.

As an example, I was told of a teacher who simply asked pupils for feedback about marking. The messages from learners were straightforward and easy to act on. The messages were:

Please do not use red pen – it ruins our work.
Please write legibly so that we can read the comments.
Please write comments that we can understand.

Simple but important and effective feedback!

Advice

Simple steps

A simple way of capturing learner voice is through the use of simple questionnaires aimed at capturing learners' perceptions of their lessons, projects, homework, resources, the type of teaching they enjoy and so on. Again any results from such questioning do not automatically confer elevated status and they do not mean that the learners, whether saying something positive or negative, are correct; but the feedback does provide information that provides the basis for rich discussion at departmental meetings and during individual discussions.

Other methods for capturing learner voice are listed below and many will already be in place – therefore an essential response to 'learner voice' is 'teacher listening'.

- Teacher dialogue in class
- Learner blogs
- Learner wikis
- Video booths
- Questionnaires
- Online surveys
- Learner posters
- Interviews
- Focus group interviews
- Student councils
- Anonymous feedback
- Pupils as researchers
- Pupil presentations
- Pupil documentaries
- Circle time
- Pupil governors
- Pupils involved in classroom observation
- Pupils as co-researchers
- Pupils evaluating work units

Activity

Just in time or just in case

All I really needed to know I learned at nursery!

It's not so much what you know but how you proceed when you don't know. For many years education has been based upon a banking mentality. The teacher deposits something with the learner hoping that it may gain some interest. Such an approach has significant limitations such as the appropriateness of what is being learned and (continuing the metaphor) the transferability of the currency, particularly using the deposited information in different contexts and at different times.

An alternative way to visualize knowledge acquisition is to use a manufacturing analogy: 'just in time' (not 'just in case'). The basis of this principle is that there is little point of having masses of skills, attitudes, concepts and knowledge 'just in case' you might one day by chance use it.

Therefore a more appropriate approach would be that you access knowledge in real time or just in time for when you need it. Ultimately what this represents is knowing how to learn – 'learning to learn' and most importantly how to proceed when you need to know something – 'self-AfL'. Such a disposition can also be conceptualized as 'catching learning' and environments have to be created in which children feel comfortable enough to do that.

Such environments already exist in many nursery schools where children are constantly in a state of connectionist and experiential learning and are learning together without even knowing – they are literally catching the learning when they need it!

Such learning is characterized by learning being the focus with assessment serving the process of learning rather than forming the focus of the learning for bureaucratic and accountability reasons.

Advice

Check what does and does not work

What does not work	What does work
Teachers assess quantity of work, presentation and perceived effort rather than the quality of learning.	Learners involved in self-assessment against agreed and shared criteria.
Most attention given to marking and grading, much of it tending to lower the self-esteem of learners, rather than to provide advice for improvement.	Providing regular feedback that leads to learners recognizing their next steps and how to take them.
Feedback to learners prioritized by managerial and accountability reasons rather than to help learners to learn more effectively.	Improving questioning technique and repertoire.
Learners compared with each other, which demoralizes the less successful learners and provides little challenge or motivation for the more successful learners.	A personal philosophy that every learner can improve.
Teachers not knowing about their learners' learning needs and not clearly understanding progression in terms of learning.	Teacher and learner dialogue to support individual next steps and inform planning.

Activity

Self-esteem and self-efficacy

It has been shown that pupils given feedback as marks are likely to see it as a way to compare themselves with other pupils, known as ego-involvement, while those given comments only see it as a means of helping them to improve. On almost all occasions the comment-only group outperform the groups given marks only. Central to this is self-esteem, possibly the single most powerful force in our existence as the way we feel and perceive ourselves affects virtually every aspect of our existence.

Self-esteem is linked to our sense of worth and is best defined as 'a confidence and satisfaction in oneself' and is closely related to a person's self-concept which relates to the 'mental image one has of oneself'. Self-esteem can therefore be considered to be a barometer for the value that a person places upon themselves.

A further linkage, which is closely related, is the concept of self-efficacy which refers to one's estimation of how well one can execute the necessary actions to deal with life events and activities including learning. The relationship among these three areas is critical as although you may have a good self-efficacy it does not follow that you also have high self-esteem or self-concept. Such an imbalance can result in an impoverished view of the self, leading to emotional disengagement and difficulties when learning – particularly when dealing with potentially negative feedback.

AfL recognizes the location of self-esteem and self-efficacy by:

> Knowing that feedback given as rewards or grades enhances ego rather than task involvement. As a consequence the learner does not improve.

> Knowing that with ego-involvement both high and low attainers are reluctant to take risks and react badly to new challenges, and that failures simply damage self-esteem.

> Knowing that with positive task-involvement, learners' self-efficacy can improve by their own effort, as they are willing to take on new challenges and to learn from failure.

No one can make you feel inferior without your consent.
Eleanor Roosevelt

Advice

BASIS (Belonging, Aspiration, Safety, Identity and Success)

The BASIS model acknowledges that without the right level of emotional support AfL is unlikely to be successful.

The BASIS model can operate at a school, class or individual level and can be used as a focus for developing a positive self-image in children through the following principles:

- Creating a sense of **Belonging** – in the sense of establishing a sense of community within a school or within a class, which includes values and celebrates with all its members.

- Creating a sense of **Aspiration** – in the sense that the environment is one that recognizes and value aspirations through sharing clear and achievable targets.

- Creating a secure environment where learners feel **Safe** – in that the learning environment is secure and emotionally safe, where diversity is valued and risk of failure is regarded as a positive and is an essential accompaniment to a challenging learning environment.

- Creating an environment which values **Identity** – in that the individuals that make up the environment are valued and where the relationship between self-esteem, self-efficacy and self-concept is central to personal development.

- Creating an environment that creates and values **Success** – in that positive stocktaking is an essential feature of successful achievement which will provide the platform for each learner to develop their lifelong abilities and aim to perform to the best of those abilities.

Activity

Motivation

I have always liked the saying 'aerodynamically speaking, bees cannot fly. It's just that they don't know it', as I believe all children can fly until we tell them they can't!

There is a classic psychological experiment in which three separate groups are asked to perform the same task. The three groups were briefed separately and asked to complete it in a set time. One group of participants were told they were being paid the equivalent of £10 for doing the task while the second group were told they would be paid the equivalent of twenty pence. The third group were asked to do the task for free: in effect it was a favour.

The group who were paid the most scored 159, while the group paid the least scored 101. These results could be as expected – except that the third group who performed the task for free scored 168, outperforming both paid groups.

The results are interesting in that they show how we rationalize according to market norms yet we are irrational when we apply social norms. The point of this in relation to AfL and motivation is clear. If we appeal to children's motivation on the basis of improving grades, scores or marks then we may only get a disproportionate response from those who perceive the gains of an appropriate value. However, presenting bigger picture gains is much more motivating – the payoff is unquantifiable and not based upon the market. This type of motivation is best described as intrinsic and is a much more powerful form of influence than external forms of motivation.

MOTIVATE

We know that intrinsic motivation is more effective than extrinsic motivation – that the implicit worth of learning is a much greater motivator than the reward of a grade or certificate. However, when dealing with a new topic it is likely that the teacher will need to make the first connections for the learner in order to emotionally engage them with a new topic. Use the model below to both plan and focus attention on building emotional engagement to develop motivation.

M – Make links for learners to a topic that has a level of emotional engagement.

O – Observe how learners respond and adjust if necessary.

T – Take time to think about further emotional connections with the topic.

I – If it is not working – adjust.

V – Verify through questions and answers learners' emotional engagement –such as how do you feel about . . . ?

A – Accept that not all learners all of the time will be emotionally engaged.

T – Think about alternative methods for emotional engagement such as visual stimuli, audio, role play narratives, hooks and WIIFM (What's In It For Me?).

E – Evaluate and adjust.

It is OK to fail, but it is not OK to give up.

Kate (aged 8)

Activity

Plenaries

AfL is woven into the fabric of the lesson – it is not added on . . .

One of the strongest features of the introduction of various national strategies over the last decade has been that they have unified language and extended teachers' vocabulary. However, in doing so they created misconceptions among teachers – most notably that every lesson consisted of three parts that began with a starter and ended with a plenary.

Plenaries have been referred to throughout this book as integral to learning; the point when you gain valuable feedback on the teaching and learning that has or has not taken place. However, a misconception is that plenaries are the 'sugar coating entertainment placed over the same old learning' when in fact they are integral to securing pupils' learning. A further misconception is that plenaries only take place at the end.

Therefore although a plenary may take place at the end of the lesson to monitor the extent to which the objectives of the lesson have been achieved, within a lesson the monitoring and re-orientation of learners will take place at regular intervals. In practice this may take the form of dividing the learning into episodes based upon the delivery of the learning objectives. Each mini-plenary would assess the extent to which learners had secured the objective before being challenged by the next objective. The mini-plenary is also a sharing point, when good practice is acknowledged and misconceptions are challenged.

A further misconception is that a plenary has to be a fun game. Although it is desirable to have fun activities, often the fun element can be seen to be overriding the learning and is part of the creeping 'edutainment' philosophy in education where learning is seen as following fun rather than the other way around.

Ultimately each mini-plenary provides a monitoring, assessment and re-orientation opportunity and as such leaving this to the end of the lesson may be too late.

Advice

Plenary ideas

- 30-second summary – learners have 30 seconds to write down and synthesize the last episode of learning.

- 1-minute summary – learners have 1 minute to write down and summarize the learning from the entire lesson.

- Text-a-friend – using text language, in 40 words explain what you have learned.

- What I didn't get – learners stick post-it notes on whiteboard space (split up for each objective) throughout the lesson, identifying what they are not understanding.

- Think-pair-share – learners agree in pairs how well they have met each objective.

- Two stars and a wish – learners feed back on two areas that have gone well and one area they need to improve upon.

- Thumbs up, thumbs across, thumbs down – used by learners when asked to indicate if they understand, not sure, didn't understand.

- True or false – quick-fire questions by teacher and learners where all learners hold up true or false statements.

- How did you feel – emotional feedback using emoticons about how the learner has felt (particularly useful when dealing with sensitive issues).

- Prioritize the objectives – learners prioritize the objectives they have most understood and least understood.

- Five quick questions – mini-plenary using targeted questions at the end of a teaching episode.

- Learners vote to decide what was least understood.

- The big questions – mini-plenary used throughout the lesson to refer back to the big question asked at the start of the lesson.

Activity

Portfolios

Increasingly portfolios are being seen as a means of viewing a learner's performance more holistically than when viewing a series of summative grades.

A key part of this is the increasing use of electronic and digital portfolios which allow large amounts of data to be centrally located yet able to be scrutinized and contributed to by a large number of interested parties including the learner, teachers, parents and carers.

This type of holistic approach changes the whole nature and dynamic of learning and assessment and moves from an atomized approach, where the learner's profile is almost insignificant, to a bigger picture of the learner's progress across a range of areas and their disposition to learning.

Unfortunately the introduction of portfolios has often been added to existing systems of accountability rather than starting from the point of how best to support learning. However, with time and the advancement of technology digital portfolios offer real opportunities for placing assessment centrally to learning, where evidence is generated in real time and where assessment is considered authentic, learner-centred and personalized.

Key features of portfolios include:

- The recognition of developmental work.

- The presentation of the learner's best work.

- The showcase for collaborative work.

- The coordination for cross-curricular work and assessment.

- The aiding of holistic assessment.

- The support of cross-curricular.

- The documentation and systematic recording of work kept by the learner but not marked.

- The process of recording ongoing work and learner self-reflection.

- The storing of multimedia materials for assessment including audio and visual materials.

Advice

Different types of portfolio to consider

Type	Uses
Personal portfolio	Records a range of activities such as community involvement, musical or artistic talents, sports, families, hobbies or travels to show the learner's wider interests, alongside school achievements. This demonstrates wider capabilities within the community which often go unacknowledged.
Best work portfolio	Learners select examples from their work across subjects. This records a learner's personal development and self-reflection. Teachers and parents can review the portfolio.
Cross-curricular assessment portfolio	By adding tags to work – work from one area of the curriculum can be viewed from another area for either content or concept. For example, creativity could be looked at by several interested parties.
Year-on-year portfolio	This personal portfolio includes learning over several school years or a key stage. Learners review the work in the portfolio and reflect upon and evaluate how much they have learned and improved over a period.
Attributes portfolio	A means for recording dispositions rather than subject disciplines.
Group work portfolio	Each member of a group contributes individual items that show individual and group strengths. This type of portfolio can be for a set period of time or cover a particular theme in any subject and encourages collaborative and cooperative work.
All of the above	The ideal portfolio would be one that contained all of the above with the different types of portfolio being filtered based upon what was being assessed.

Activity

4

The big picture

Teacher constructs

The truth, as if you didn't know, is that the assessment of learning is not an exact science and often we can be very wrong but this will largely depend upon the personal construct we adopt. A starting point is to think of your position and how you see your role. So do you see yourself as:

a. **A Distributor** – you distribute grades to children. So my role is simply to give out grades based upon my experience.

b. **An Allocator** – you allocate children to different social groups (not just attainment). So, won't achieve much, high flyer, loser.

c. **A Hiker** – no matter the child you aim to hike the child up. You work out where a child is in their learning and move from one step to the next, constantly providing them with the next challenge.

Hopefully your answer is (c) but there are lots of a's and b's in the teaching profession who are what we can call 'schoolers' rather than 'educators'. The difference is that a 'schooler' does not add value to the child and sees their role as clarifying a child's particular station in life. The 'educators' believe that children have unlimited potential and are always providing the next challenge. Fundamental to this is assessment and whether you see it as a tool to tell children where they are and hope they get better or as a tool to tell them where they have just left and where they are heading.

Advice

AfL is a broad concept that links to a whole range of teaching and learning strategies. Perhaps the ultimate challenge that teachers face, however, is a personal one in how the teacher conceives the learning environment.

Teacher construct

Taking time to reflect upon your personal construct is important as without knowing what we prioritize we cannot make decisions about how to change or improve practice. By listing our assessment, pedagogical and subject priorities we can start to reflect upon what our personal construct is. In each box in Figure 4.1 list your priorities and see how your construct develops.

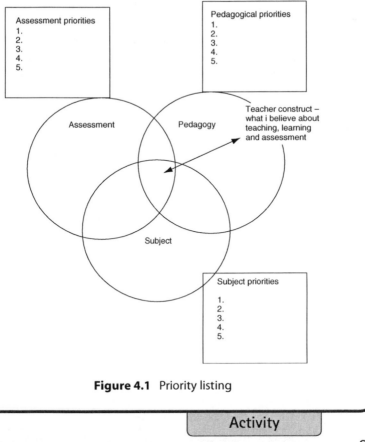

Figure 4.1 Priority listing

Activity

Formative use of summative assessment

Human beings like measuring – It must be a deeply evolutionary thing inside us all as part of our survival mechanism – but it doesn't mean it is always good to measure or compare!

I often think the medical equivalent of the way schools use assessment is that of a patient visiting a doctor: while the doctor tells the patient what is wrong with them they don't always tell the patient how to get better. Schools have a long tradition of gathering summative assessment information – presumably this mass of data could be collated and coordinated and used very powerfully. However, many teachers and schools do not use the available summative information in a formative way – as a means of informing about the nature and quality of teaching and learning and to use such information to adjust future teaching in an attempt to improve learning.

In many ways summative assessments have received a lot of bad press – but this is often because we know that the reliability and validity of certain types of assessment are limited. However the formative use of good summative assessment data (tests, homework, etc.) can provide valuable information.

What is more, if the thousands and thousands of bits of data that are generated by teacher marking were coordinated in some way through the use of technology across the school then this really would provide an effective snapshot of a where a child's learning is at, which could then be used to shape, adjust and refine future teaching.

For such data to be really effective the quality of assessment must be robust and the information generated must be available to be used formatively by the learner.

Advice

Formative use of summative assessment

The following is a list of different ways in which coordinated summative assessments can be analysed and used formatively to improve learning and performance. The emphasis is not to use the information to label a learner, but to use the information to enhance learner performance through the effective formative use of accumulated data:

At a school level:

- analysing the difference between boys' and girls' performance
- analysing the attainment of children of different ethnic origin
- analysing different teacher performance with similar groups
- analysing different subject performance
- analysing correlations between performance and other factors, for example, attendance
- analysis and monitoring different interventions such as curriculum developments
- analysing performance across years and year-on-year performance.

At a learner level:

- tracking learner progress in and across subjects
- tracking learner performance across years
- monitoring generic skills and concepts across subjects
- tracking the learner's trajectory across a key stage
- identifying learning difficulties across subjects
- identifying impact of intervention activities upon specific learners
- establishing a holistic view of learner performance and progress
- specific question-level analysis for individual learners
- generating specific diagnostic information for individual learners to enhance future learning and teaching.

Activity

Findings from research into AfL

AfL is more than not giving a number. It is about helping learners progress.

Most teachers will have at least heard of and possibly read *Inside the Black Box* written by Dylan Wiliam and Paul Black (1998). This small booklet has become one of the most influential publications in education, drawing upon research to influence practice. The pamphlet summarizes the main findings from 250 assessment articles based upon nine years of international research related to assessment and synthesizes this material into a manageable format.

The black box metaphor represents the systems approach that is often used as a reductionist method of education – such that you put *x* in and you get *y* out – when in reality education, schools, teachers and learners are much more complex than this. The book therefore takes interaction and dialogue as central to learning and from the research three main points emerged:

First, formative assessment really does improve standards. Second, there is a need to improve teachers' practice related to assessment and learning in the classroom related to formative approaches. Third, do we know how to make it work? The unequivocal answer was yes.

Wiliam and Black stress, however, that there cannot be any quick fix as AfL is more than a single set of strategies and is more a philosophy of learning and teaching, developed over a period of time.

Advice

AfL research headlines

Weaknesses of current assessment systems:

- The propensity to value quantity and presentation rather than the quality of learning.

- Lowering self-esteem of learners by over-concentrating on summative judgements rather than advice for improvement of learning.

- Lowering self-esteem of learners by comparing them negatively and repeatedly with more successful learners.

- Giving feedback that serves bureaucratic and managerial purposes rather than helping learners to learn more effectively.

- Teachers tend to work with an incomplete picture of pupils' learning needs.

Five key factors that improve learning through assessment:

- Providing effective feedback to learners.

- Actively involving learners in their own learning.

- Adjusting teaching, often in real time, to take account of the results of assessment.

- Recognizing the significant influence assessment has on the motivation and self-esteem of learners.

- Recognizing the need for learners to be able to assess themselves and to understand how to improve.

Good AfL:

- is embedded, rather than bolted on, to teaching and is part of a change of personal philosophy and school culture.

- involves sharing the learning with pupils.

- enables learners to know and recognize the standards they are aiming for.

- involves learners in self-assessment.

Activity

Developing whole school approach to AfL

As previously indicated, AfL is much more than a set of tactics to improve learner attainment. Ultimately it is a philosophy about both what and how children learn. Equally, while a school may start off with a few interested individuals delivering AfL (perhaps, reader, you are the fortunate one), eventually the approach will be best developed across the whole school.

This can only be done by developing a genuine understanding of how AfL works and engaging colleagues in a conversation about learning. This also needs parents to understand the concepts that underlie the methods involved in AfL as well learners understanding their part in the development of the strategy.

AfL cannot, however, exist on its own as it relies upon professional development and professional dialogue about learning as well as peer support and coaching to underpin its development and refinement. All of this requires that most precious commodity in schools – time – and unless given sufficient time it will not be a success. However, the aims and principles of AfL are so laudable that it is difficult to argue against their inclusion.

As a starting point – use the activity below to identify where you are and how you need to progress.

Advice

Where are we?

Use the card exercise below with colleagues to identify where you are and what stage you are at. Place the cards in priority order by negotiating what are your subject, faculty or school priorities.

AfL is recognized as central to good classroom practice – Where are we?	AfL focuses on how students learn – Where are we?
AfL is part of effective planning of teaching and learning – Where are we?	AfL is regarded as a key professional skill for teachers – Where are we?
AfL takes account of the importance of learner motivation – Where are we?	AfL is sensitive and constructive because any assessment has an emotional impact – Where are we?
AfL promotes commitment to learning goals and a shared understanding of the criteria by which they are assessed – Where are we?	Learners receive constructive guidance about how to improve – Where are we?
AfL recognizes the full range of achievements of all learners – Where are we?	AfL develops learners' capacity for self-assessment so that they can become reflective and self-managing – Where are we?

Activity

Autonomy not automation – comment-only feedback

Perhaps one of the most contentious issues in the use of AfL is the use of comment-only marking as one part of the strategy. For many teachers this is the 'bridge too far' day prompting the diehards in the staffroom to begin the 'inmates are running the asylum' routine or the 'you don't have to be mad to work here, but it helps' repertoire.

So why does this concept generate such consternation among so many teachers?

Quite simply because it is more challenging and time consuming if it is done correctly – however, it is equally more formative and productive again if done correctly.

A misconception is that comment-only marking is therefore a replacement for all existing marking – it isn't. Comment-only marking is supported by teacher and pupil discussion, peer-to-peer discussions, learner self-assessments and ongoing summative type marking. Comment-only marking is therefore part of a collection of methods in which the teacher uses their professional judgement to decide when each is best used.

It is particularly interesting that the subject that has often struggled most with comment-only marking is the mathematics community – even though AfL very much grew out of the that community. The big change is that for comment-only marking to be really effective you have to consider what you are asking – if the question is simply a one-correct-answer response then you would most likely continue to mark in the same way. However, if your questions and tasks open up and challenge thinking then the feedback can be much more formative.

One final misconception is that any comment will do. So in many cases teachers have replaced a tick with a word – such as good or wrong. This is a summative comment when the ideal scenario is that the comment provokes further thinking, and identifies the source of difficulties as well as pointing the learner in the right direction.

Advice

Adjust or accept?

This is an activity which illustrates a way of using comment-only marking along with peer-to-peer assessment.

Learners work on an activity – perhaps an ongoing project of some sort.

The criteria for the assessment of the activity will have been negotiated prior to the exercise starting.

At interim stages (not just at the end) learners peer-assess each other's work in a conveyor belt style – so they assess someone's work and move it on.

When learners are peer-assessing they are writing on a Post-it note two areas for improvement and one thing they liked (against the criteria), which they stick on the work.

After going through several assessments the work goes back to the owner – adorned with several Post-it notes.

The owner of the work then completes the (scaled down) example sheet below stating whether they accept the comments or whether they feel the comments need amending – if they feel it has been incorrectly assessed against the criteria, or interpreted incorrectly.

The teacher then comment-only marks the Amend or Accept sheet (not the actual work) feeding back and moderating the comments, indicating whether the comments were fair or whether the adjustment was needed or necessary. This means the teacher is honing the learners' reflective skills rather than focusing purely on the work.

Accept or Amend?

Place Post-it note 1 here	I accept or amend – why?
	Teacher comment:

(Continued)

Activity

97

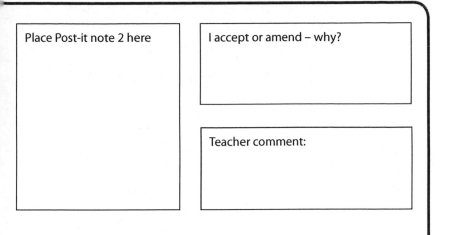

Place Post-it note 2 here	I accept or amend – why?
	Teacher comment:

Place Post-it note 3 here	I accept or amend – why?
	Teacher comment:

Communicating learning expectations – what and should you share?

There is plenty of debate about objectives and outcomes and how they should be expressed. However simple definitions of both would be:

Objectives – These are what the teacher intends learners to learn . . . Today you will learn X (based upon a skill, attitude, concept or knowledge). Also sometimes referred to as learning goals or learning intentions.

Outcomes – These are how achievement will be demonstrated by the learner. As a result of learning X you will be able to – followed by an active/measurable verb followed by what they will be able to do.

Assessment can be defined as:

Assessment – I will know you are able to do X by assessing your outcomes using (followed by the assessment method and sharing and negotiation of criteria) . . .

Why the fuss and distinction? Well, I have seen many teachers suddenly realize how simple yet effective this can all be when the penny has dropped and they recognize the distinction and need for the different areas.

Should I be sharing the objectives and outcomes and if so how? As always there are different principles to this. First, there is no point sharing if you are not committed to the process. Second, certain creative activities would lose some of their validity by sharing the outcomes as this could overly distort a creative response. Third, the objectives/outcomes you write for yourself may be slightly different from those you would share – so there is a certain amount of adapting in order that they can be fully understood by the learner.

Finally, a fear I have with all the national strategies is that everything becomes very similar in every lesson. All the national strategies and initiatives are baseline material. If your lessons are better by maintaining the principles but doing it in a different way and most importantly effective learning is taking place – then do it your way!

Advice

Objectives checklist

- Are the objectives and outcomes displayed throughout the lesson – so the learners can see what the learning focus and outcomes are?

- Do you regularly return to the objectives throughout the lesson signposting which objective is currently being delivered?

- Is the lesson delivered in chunks/learning episodes based upon each objective?

- Are the objectives and outcomes written in learner language appropriate for the age of the learner?

- Are signals sent from the teacher to the learner when moving from one lesson objective to another?

- Are the objectives expressed in terms of learning and not what the learners will be doing?

- Are the outcomes expressed as what the learners will be able to do as a result of the learning?

- Have the criteria for assessing the outcomes been shared/discussed/negotiated/highlighted?

- Are learners involved in generating success criteria for meeting the objectives?

- Has space been created for learners to self-assess or peer-assess their achievement against the objectives?

Activity

Peer review/coaching

Implementing a variety of strategies for AfL is not really that tricky. Embedding them as part of a concerted effort to put AfL at the centre of teaching and learning is a different matter. To do this may require change in teacher practice as well as organizational and institutional changes. This is why research on the extent to which practice is being changed can be quite disappointing as the same features are constantly reported where AfL isn't working.

These include:

- emphasis on tranmissionist approaches to learning

- a tendency for teachers to reward presentation and quantity

- over-emphasis on marking and grading of learners

- lessons planned with AfL strategies added rather than embedded in the teaching and learning

- objectives shared but something else is assessed.

If teaching is to change then teachers need support to do so and increasingly schools are identifying coaches who can help colleagues develop their teaching repertoire and philosophy to engage with AfL principles. Such coaching and peer review is critical in supporting the development of AfL in schools and most importantly embedding it into practice. As part of this it is important that teachers recognize that implementing AfL is an ongoing process of refinement. It is not a quick fix and therefore the use of coaching and peer observations as part of a dialogue of improvement is central to good practice.

Advice

AfL observation guide

AfL Peer Lesson Observation	
Introduction/Starter	
Engaging start, rich context Learning objectives are shared with learners Learning outcomes are clearly communicated Time frames for chunks of learning identified Why we are learning x is placed in clear context The 'big picture' is clear Homework if given presented at the start to provide a focus for the learning	Comment:
Teaching and learning episodes	
Criteria are exemplified and pupils involved in generating criteria Teacher models and 'scaffolds' the learning Learning remains focused on the learning objectives A range of teaching and teaching strategies are employed Opportunities are built in to lesson to engage all pupils in dialogue Learners are encouraged to reflect on their learning Teacher adapts lesson based upon feedback	Comment:
Questioning episodes	
A variety of strategies employed A variety of question styles used Targeted and pre planned questions employed High level questions (Bloom's) Teacher employs appropriate 'wait time' for questions	Comment:

(Continued)

Activity

Advice

	Comment:
Think-pair-share No hands Teacher avoids 'signalling' answer when appropriate Questions relate to the learning objectives/ outcomes Questions provoke and challenge misconceptions	
Learner outcomes	
	Comment:
Learners engaged by content, pace and style of lesson Learners have opportunity to reflect upon own progress Learners assessed against objectives Learner opportunity for feedback (e.g. traffic lights)	

	Comment:
Teacher feedback	
Learning objectives used as basis for feedback Teacher uses comment-only Learners have opportunity to read and set targets based upon feedback Learners emotional needs considered	
Plenary/end	
	Comment:
Plenary relates to learning objectives and outcomes Learning progress is celebrated Teacher identifies learner targets for next lesson	

Activity

Changing attitudes and expectations – reframing

We are all creatures of habit and we dislike change; before long, routines become expectations which are difficult to break. So even though you may be fired up to introduce or extend AfL – don't expect the same reaction from colleagues, pupils and parents.

> *You mean you don't put your hand up if you know*
> *the answer – that's just daft ...*

However, the evidence shows that experienced teachers can adjust their practice with overwhelming effect. Equally children's comments from research carried out in schools that have adopted AfL show a profound insight and a realization that this offers much more than the mystique of 'guess what's inside the teacher's head'.

Education is a triangular relationship between the school, the learner and the home and convincing parents of the benefits of AfL are an important part of its development and promotion in schools. Therefore involving parents and carers as co-educators of their children is important.

Essential to all this is reframing what it means to learn and how we learn.

AfL is not just about doing what we currently do with a few extra bits. It is about rethinking how children learn, how it is best to learn and ultimately what is better for learners in terms of developing a lifelong disposition towards learning.

Advice

Involving parents and carers

While schools create policies for developing AfL, it is important that parents and carers are also involved in this process. Some possible ideas:

- get learners to create a parents' guide to AfL
- create a glossary of terms for the school prospectus
- invite parents to participate in observing lessons
- run an AfL evening
- VLE video clips of AfL in practice
- links to teachers' TV online so that they can see AfL in action
- run a mock lesson with parents as learners
- create a guide for how parents can use AfL strategies when supporting their child's learning at home.

In doing all of this it is important that any guidance:

- explains why AfL is used in a school
- explains in 'parent/carer-friendly' language how AfL looks in classrooms, what they may see (as in homework and feedback) and hear (as in what their children say) that is different
- suggests opportunities in which parents and carers can support their child's learning at home adopting the using AfL principles (e.g. structuring the learning and not doing the child's work for them).

Activity

Working collaboratively

A simple aim of AfL – Pupils working harder than the teacher.

Increasing the learner's autonomy and ownership as part of AfL also increases learner accountability – this means that learners have to take responsibility for participation and collaborative working. In many schools a misconception can exist between collaborative work and group work and a useful method for encouraging collaboration is the PIES approach. Based around four areas, the PIES approach works on the principle of maximum and equal participation and responsibility of all learners. This means that although working in a group, individuals cannot hide as there is both individual accountability and group responsibility based upon equal participation. PIES includes the following:

Positive Interdependence (a structured activity that requires a group to complete the task)

Individual Accountability (individual contribution with the task is also identifiable and accountable)

Equal Participation (everyone contributes and takes turns)

Simultaneous Interaction (all participants are active – if not speaking then listening).

PIES combines an encouragement of AfL principles with a strategy that enhances collaborative work in a more advanced way by encouraging participation strategies.

If these four basic principles are in place, it represents good cooperative learning – if not it is merely disparate group work.

Advice

Collaborative contracts

When working collaboratively it is worth investing time for the learners to generate a contract for how they will participate and contribute. It is really important that the contract is generated by the group; however, a guide might include:

Group partnerships agreement	
Names	
1.	2.
3.	4.
Here are our agreed rules about participation:	
1.	
2.	
3	
When we are feeding back to each other we will:	
When assessing each other's ideas our five golden rules will be:	
Respect our partner(s)' work because they have done their best and so their work should be valued.	
Try to see how they have tackled the learning objective and only try to improve things that are to do with the learning objective.	
Tell our partner(s) the good things we see in their work.	
Try to make our suggestions as clear as possible.	
Be fair to our partner(s). We will not talk about their work behind their backs because we wouldn't like them to do it to us.	

Activity

Assessment reform group – ten principles for AfL

1. AfL should be part of effective planning of teaching and learning.

2. AfL should focus on how students learn.

3. AfL should be recognized as central to classroom practice.

4. AfL should be regarded as a key professional skill for teachers.

5. AfL should be sensitive and constructive because any assessment has an emotional impact.

6. AfL should take account of the importance of learner motivation.

7. AfL should promote commitment to learning goals and a shared understanding of the criteria by which they are assessed.

8. Learners should receive constructive guidance about how to improve.

9. AfL develops learners' capacity for self-assessment so that they can become reflective and self-managing.

10. AfL should recognize the full range of achievements of all learners.

Advice

Diamond 9

At this stage, hopefully you recognize both the enormity and the significant opportunity that AfL presents. However it cannot be tackled in one go. Therefore a useful tool for prioritizing action is the diamond 9 tool below which, by completing from top to bottom, helps you decide and work though your priorities in implementing AfL.

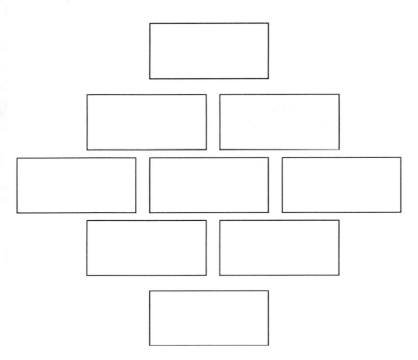

Figure 4.2 Diamond 9 tool

Self-evaluation – where are we?

Nearly there! We are almost at the end so it is time to reflect on where you are.

The table opposite is adapted from the national strategy and is a useful means of identifying your starting point with AfL. It has been deliberately placed at the back of the book as, having read the book, hopefully you are in a better position to evaluate where you are and what you need to consider next.

For many the concept of AfL is a difficult one, particularly as you are possibly being asked to challenge the construct of teaching and learning that you hold. It is even more difficult as questioning involves unpicking your own success – presumably you were a success with traditional educational approaches and it didn't do you any harm. Equally your decision to become a teacher was presumably based on a model of teaching that you had experienced as a learner.

Therefore the change in philosophy and approach is not an easy one. However, moving away from receptive and passive transmissionist notions of teaching towards connectionist and constructivist approaches with built-in assessment, in real time, has to be the way forward.

The decision to adapt is therefore a purely professional one!

Advice

Self-evaluation – are we there yet?

Elements of AfL	Focusing	Developing	Establishing	Enhancing
• Conditions for learning • The use of curricular targets • Designing opportunities for learning (planning) • Strategies for day-to-day assessment in the classroom • Feedback on learning • Involving parents and carers • The formative use of summative assessment	At this stage, the school recognizes that it is at the beginning of a process. The school identifies what is already happening but recognizes that much remains to be done.	At the developing stage, the school has started to develop some of the aspects of AfL, but there is a need for further development to secure and consolidate practice.	At this stage, there still remain some issues to address in terms of whole school consistency and cohesion but many things are now in place and are becoming embedded. There have been some significant developments on the quality of provision and a real impact on standards.	At this stage, the identified aspects of the AfL are embedded fully in whole-school approaches and practice. There is whole school consistency and cohesive practice. The impact on standards and progress is evident.
	Key steps to progress to developing stage? 1 2 3	Key steps to progress to establishing stage? 1 2 3	Key steps to progress to enhancing stage? 1 2 3	Key steps to maintaining enhancing stage? 1 2 3

Activity

113

References and further reading

This book has presented a snapshot of AfL and you are encouraged to tap into the wealth of literature that is appearing on the topic to further extend your understanding. Below is a list of good resources which will further extend your understanding of the powerful concept of AfL.

Assessment Reform Group (2002), *Assessment for Learning: 10 Principles. Research-Based Principles to Guide Classroom Practice*. Leaflet/poster available at http://www.assessment-reform-group.org/CIE3.PDF (website address checked 01.02.2009).

Black, P., Harrison, C., Lee, C., Marshall, B. and Wiliam, D. (2003), *AfL: Putting It into Practice*. Milton Keynes: Open University Press.

Black, P. and Wiliam, D. (1998), *Inside the Black Box: Raising Standards Through Classroom Assessment*. London, Kings College: Assessment for Learning Group.

Department for Children, Schools and Families (DfCSF) (2008), *The Children's Plan: Building Brighter Futures*. London: TSO.

Haney, W. (1991), 'We must take care: Fitting assessments to functions', in V. Perrone (ed.), *Expanding Student Assessment*. Alexandria, VA: Association for Supervision and Curriculum Development, pp. 142–163.

Holt, J. (1995), *How Children Fail* (Classics in Child Development). New York: Da Capo Press.

James, M., Wiliam, D. and Southworth, G. (2005), 'Learning how to learn in classrooms, schools and networks: teaching and learning research programme (phase II)'. ESRC project.

Klenowski, V. (2002), *Developing Portfolios for Learning and Assessment: Processes and Principles*. London: Routledge.

Teachernet.gov.uk (2008), 'The AfL Strategy', in http://publications.teachernet. gov.uk. Enter in search box DCSF-00341-2008.

Tomlinson, C. A. (2008), *The Parallel Curriculum: A Design to Develop Learner Potential and Challenge Advanced Learners* (second edn). Thousand Oaks, CA: Corwin Press.